lives
less
ordinary

lives less ordinary

Thirty-two Irish portraits

JUDY KRAVIS
&
PETER MORGAN

The Lilliput Press, Dublin

First published 1999 by The Lilliput Press Ltd, 62–63 Sitric Road, Arbour Hill, Dublin 7, Ireland. E-mail: lilliput@indigo.ie. Web site: http://indigo.ie/~lilliput.

A CIP record for this title is available from the British Library.

ISBN 1 901866 22 x

The authors wish to acknowledge the financial support of University College Cork, and of the county councils of Cork, South Dublin, Kildare and Offaly.

The Lilliput Press receives financial assistance from An Chomhairle Ealaíon / The Arts Council of Ireland.

Set in 11.5 on 15 Adobe Garamond. Printed in Ireland by Betaprint of Clonshaugh, Dublin.

Contents

contents   8

Introduction

The people we talked to for this book have all made unusual choices. They've done different, as Carmel Duffy says. They're content not to feel part of the mainstream. For many the choices were dramatic – or so their friends told them! They have given up jobs, careers, and sometimes the habits of generations. In our conversations they reflected on the lives they lead, the work they do and how well they like it.

The process of finding them was serendipitous and organic: chance encounters, suggestions from friends, hearsay. One black beetle knows another, as Patrick Lydon says. These are not people who seek to proselytize – they don't necessarily want more people like themselves in the world. Andy Warhol's prediction that soon everyone would be famous for fifteen minutes is far from their thinking. Their lives are outwardly quiet; their houses do not shout at the passer-by, and they do not seek to make headlines.

Although their lives may be lived at a tangent to the mainstream of our society, they are not cut off from it. They all buy and sell to some degree. They produce. But they don't worship money. By the way they live and work they show a scepticism about those social structures that attempt to control them. Frequently they set up their own structures, like community co-ops and home schools. Most of them create their own employment and work at home, or close by. Most produce things with their hands. What they produce is integral to their lives, as well as a source of freedom and pleasure.

Many of these people make us think of a past we know or wish we knew. A past is what you can mentally encompass, it has a wholeness the present seems to lack. It's hard to interfere with the past. A family of travelling people, a Camphill community, a hermit, present a simplicity that looks utopian – a memorial to the past or a blueprint for the future – unless you're living in it, in which case it's simply life.

Many of them live on the land. Some are willing solitaries, who like their own company; for them solitude is not a black hole, it's a daily pleasure. Some want to change society, actively, as well as by the example of the way they live. Some live a simple life because they always have and it suits them. Joey Block, woodcutter on his own patch, knows where to put such of the modern world as does not meet his case – out the door.

Our conversations with the people in this book often stretched over several days. The portraits are edited transcripts of their words – with the exception of two or three cases where a tape recorder would have been intrusive. As each portrait records a particular moment in a person's life, we have chosen not to indicate the changes that have taken place since we met them.

This book is a tribute as well as an exploration. In the late twentieth century it is a great achievement to walk to a different drummer. There's so much din from society's big drum. Fifty years ago in Ireland there were hedge teachers who went from place to place teaching, playing music, telling stories. The people in this book are the hedge teachers of our day; they pop up out of the blue, they represent no one except themselves, and then there they are, gone.

Judy Kravis
Inniscarra, Co. Cork

Marcus and Kate McCabe, with their two children Tyrone (Toto) and Róisín, are creating a permaculture centre, The Whole Ark, on eight acres of former bog land on the Monaghan–Fermanagh border. We talked to Marcus.

The problem is the solution

I grew up around here, right on the border. County Fermanagh is across the other side of the pond – and it's directly south! And over there to the east is the South, if you see what I mean. We're here about three or four years now. We were two years up in my father's old home, up the mountain, near Lacky Bridge – the one that was always blocked, that got all the publicity. It took us an hour to travel three miles to visit the parents. The military presence, the whole atmosphere of the North, of the border, you become aware of it from when you're a small child. Toto used to be terrified of the helicopters.

If you go half a mile from here there are three guards standing waiting for mad cows to come in from the North. And that's another story: the beginning and the end of agriculture, and it's probably been coming for an awful long time. The land is almost derelict. Policy is incoherent, when you look at headage payments, and soil erosion from overpopulation of sheep. There's a war on the resources of the planet. I was in a place in Sligo yesterday, and a hedge had been taken out and burned. There was enough timber in it to keep a masonry stove burning for about three years. No value is placed on things. It's easier to go down and buy a bag of coal than to go to the trouble of cutting up the wood.

The land lacks people. The kids go away to the city, because the parents are struggling to make a living; those same children are still supported by land; the food is there for them in supermarkets, but the connection is completely obscured. So we're looking at ways in which people can either move onto the land and make a living, or stay on the land, which means looking at the way land is owned.

The international permaculture convergence four years ago was in Scandinavia. We were on a farm in Norway where the line of father and son went back to the year 800 in an unbroken line – father to eldest son. Primogeniture is the basis of our legal system. There's a real hatred of farms being split up in Ireland, it goes back to the Famine, and the penal laws; you had to divide land equally among your children. Before that, land was owned collectively, by clans, and people had a licence to use land, or to move animals through land, like pigs or geese. I think we can set up systems like that now. People can collectively buy land, own their house, their garden, and then have access to commonage, which is managed collectively. Talking about land reform is crazy. People fight wars over that sort of thing.

If you have two hundred acres of land owned by forty or fifty families, then all the milk that's produced supplies everybody within that community. And the shit from those cows can go on to someone else's business, like energy production. Start making connections between the people and the livestock and the plants within a system. Two hundred acres is a huge area and can produce a lot of food. I would create land trusts, so that the land is owned by a trust in perpetuity, and is governed by elders who are elected to be responsible towards that land, whether it's eight acres or a thousand acres. The trust can lease out homes long-term, so you're not going to be evicted. You have your garden, but you have access to other land as well, so that you can fly bees through it, or run geese through it, or sheep. An awful lot of resources can be produced: food, timber, roofing, the bulk materials for building. Monasteries have always done that, and they've always been prosperous; because there are more people, they can make much better use of the land resources.

I run courses here on how to do all that. Different sorts of people come on the courses: people who are stuck in the cities, people who are living in the country and don't really know what to do, people who have come across the idea of permaculture and think it's generally brilliant anyway. And then there's teaching by example.

There's a farmer up the road who comes down to look at what we're doing. He'll probably look for another two or three years before he makes a decision. He's got cows, and he's realizing that's coming to an end. He keeps bees, he generates his own electricity, he's got good respect for his land. He's told that alfalfa doesn't grow in Ireland, but he's got some from us and it's growing fantastically; so he's wondering why they're saying it doesn't grow here. He's very interested in trees. He's considering getting rid of his cows and getting goats, and he's looking into how to set up a forage system for goats, so they're not just getting grass, but also tree boughs, and everything that's coming down from the trees.

He's willing to experiment, and I think he's not so rare. There are quite a few like him, dotted about the landscape. You come across them when you start a place like this. They notice you and they come in. My own father was inclined to experiment on the farm in the early years, but the environment was very unfavourable to organics in the fifties and six-ties. While I was studying horticulture at UCD, I grew three acres of rasp-berries and half an acre of strawberries up at my parents' place. I hate to admit it, but I was using sprays and fertilizers; that was what was done then. As time went on I could see what was happening: the structure of the soil deteriorated rapidly, there was a lack of life. But they taught you in col-lege that everything was going to die and rot if you didn't use sprays.

In the library at UCD I discovered all this information about what fertilizers were doing to the soil, and the damage pesticides were doing on a global scale. We weren't taught any of that at college, no, no, no, no, not at all. Then in my final year I organized a debate on organics. It was packed, mostly with academics, even old retired ones had been wheeled out, it was very very heated and lively. That was a landmark for me. I start-ed thinking about fertility and what that actually is. Why do we have to pour so much into a farm in order to get anything out at all? How is it that a forest can just grow and grow and grow, just create more and more of itself?

After I left college I got a job in third-level education, which I could have stayed in till I was sixty-five and had a very easy life. But my con-science wouldn't let me teach these lads how to spray and how to fertilize their monocultures, and my bosses wouldn't let me teach anything else. I remember sitting in my office surrounded by all these books about fertiliz-

the problem is the solution

ers and pesticides, and thinking, I can't do this, I can't do this – I almost get indigestion thinking about it. My parents were absolutely horrified: I was giving up a good job, and signing on, and what was I thinking about?

I became a campaigner for Earthwatch, and did a lot of trying to get media attention: dumping manure outside the Department of Agriculture, and bringing coffins to the Dáil. I did that for about three years and got very burnt out. You might get a couple of column inches in the *Irish Times*, but nobody really seemed to care, and nobody seemed to be offering alternatives. At that stage I came across permaculture. I found two books sitting on the shelves at the Centre for Alternative Technology, and I remember flipping through the books and being completely amazed. How to set up Eden in your own place. I couldn't understand why it wasn't being shouted from the rooftops. Permaculture is a natural system, it's like the human garden extended. You're building up the relationships between plants, animals, and all the other living things in the biosphere are working together to create something we can use – or not use.

Permaculture is about how things are placed. The fact that our vegetable garden is immediately outside our kitchen is not an accident: you go out, pick your meal, bring it in and make it. We made that lake out there. This was a bog, an unusable field. So we dug out a lake, we made dry land on which to build a house, and we've raised the water table – I'm very proud of that. You've got all these wetlands being drained all over Ireland. The problem is the solution. You've got wet land, well, that's the solution, keep it wet, make it wetter. We've loads of rain, so dig out ponds, get rid of the mad cows and eat a bit more fish. The lake reflects light onto that back wall in the wintertime; you're getting 80 per cent reflected light, and on a frosty, clear day, it's warm in the middle of the day in the house. The geese range through and keep all the mulch plants down among the fruit trees. They mix in very well. The pig is a rotavator. All these things come together as a system.

Our plan is that this building we're in now will be the teaching building, it won't be our house. We're going to build a straw-bale house next year, so we can do more courses here. We want to move in the direction of an eco-village, so that more people can live here, owning their own houses. I was in a rural college in Draperstown recently, which has about two or three million in funding. I was really interested; it sounded as if they were doing what needed to be done: setting up a model. It was a hundred and fifty acres of forest, and well-architected buildings with courtyards and restaurants, but not so much as a chive, not a lettuce, not an animal. If you come to our place to do a course, you're going to be fed from the garden. It's important for people to see that we're living from what we grow, that we have a good life, we're warm, the water's hot, and the work is very diverse. You don't have to work hard, but you're very busy.

We're taught from an early age to tolerate drudgery, sitting still for six hours and learning things by heart, when actually playing is learning. Children instinctively play and learn what adults do. When we're playing we're learning. Adults too. Play and learn what children do! Play at what you like doing. People need to know what they want to do, what they like doing, what they enjoy doing, what they would pooter and footer at if they had lots of time to themselves. I love pottering around in the polytunnel. I love digging, sawing, building, planting, contact with animals – I love talking!

So many people find it hard to know what they like doing. The media create such a clutter you can't hear yourself. And we can distract ourselves so easily. If there's a television in the room, it deadens everything. We've a neighbour who calls in here to get away from the television in his own house. He sits here and smokes his pipe, and if there's nothing to be said he doesn't say anything. That's a real country thing. It's like the giant in Oscar Wilde. The selfish giant went to meet another giant down in Cornwall, and he left after seven years because they ran out of conversation. It was a long conversation but it came to an end. So he left.

the problem is the solution

Joe O'Mahony (a.k.a. Joey Block) fells trees, cuts planks, sells firewood and makes children's hurley sticks. He's always on the lookout for a good ash tree.

Here's Joey Block

The way I look at it is this: the world's a jigsaw and people are all comical items in it. Here's Joey Block down at Ardrum with his wife Bernadette and four children – three boys at home and the girl, she's married in Cork – as well as, at the last count, eleven cats, four dogs, Minnie the goat and Alfie the sheep. Here's small Joey on his patch where he's reared his family these thirty-two years – how I got here, that's a fairy tale – third-generation woodcutter, Joey works on his patch of ground, keeping away quiet and original, when the big guys attack!

He lets the word rest, he lets it travel around his land, his trees, his sheds, his machines, down the lane he picked and shovelled himself in 1958.

And listen to me here, d'you know what I said to the big guys? I said, you come in here with your machines and you'll have to mow through the six of us. And I went to the priest and I said: You've got room for six coffins in here, haven't you? The family's reared and Joey's going nowhere. I said to the big guys, you're not just taking on Joe Block, you're taking on a wife and family.

The big guys were trying to knock his trees, widen his stream; he was part of their scheme and they were not part of his. He took them to court; he called twenty-seven witnesses and would have brought in Minnie the goat; he spoke his own defence, and won – and he's proud.

If you had a man with the book-learning standing right here now and he saw the family that's grown now and the hill behind with that sun on it, would he say that Joe and his family should be moved on up the Tower road so the big guys can complete their scheme? He would not. And neither would the man up there. If there was a man up there. D'you believe in the man up there?

I'll tell you now how I came here. I came out with the wife and the wife's mother, just out in the car for a drive one Sunday in 1958. We stopped at the post office to buy – I can remember exactly what we bought – one of those chocolate things, and I asked was there any handy cottage about that was empty? The old fella in there said to go out the door and turn left then left again and up the lane – I told you it was a fairy tale – and in the end we were given the cottage with the bit of land – no paper, no signatures, no agreements. And we came in and reared the family. Thirty-two years. I fall the trees and I make the hurleys, and I don't want anything only to keep things going as they are.

Alfie! *he calls to the sheep who's tied to a tree down the lane.* Alfie! He usually answers. *On the third call, Alfie does.*

Alice Maher is a painter. She grew up on a farm in County Tipperary, and currently lives in an oval room in a Dublin square.

You know the way

You know the way in school you always get left in charge because you're the biggest girl in the class – people believe you when you're big. I had independence foisted upon me. I went to Spain when I was sixteen to be an *au pair*, and I went on my own, changing planes and so on; this didn't seem to be a problem for me, yet my sister Christine, who was small and had been sickly as a child, had to be driven everywhere. So I think it began when I took on the mantle of responsibility. I didn't like it – I don't like it now – but every family needs a safety-valve and in our family that was me, someone in whom the others can invest their wishes for freedom, a boiling pot.

I was never ever afraid of anything in my whole life. I don't think about putting down roots or being older and sicker. I prefer the insecurity, if that's what it is; that's the way I live best. When I made the decision to go to art college, I trusted that the money would come. And it usually has. I didn't really *choose* to be not married, not in a house, not having a job. It wasn't out of defiance. I've just been really busy! It's as if I arrived here at this age very quickly. I don't remember what happened in my twenties. You know how it is, you wander round the world, money-making, dope-smoking, hitchhiking, living in tents. I'm thirty-eight now, going on thirty-nine, and I've never owned anything – except a car, for a while. I'd like to own a car again, I like mobility. The minute I buy a house the trouble will start! That must be the way it was meant to be for me.

I never made the decision to be an artist; there's nothing as bad as deciding 'I want to be an artist.' I'd never met an artist when I was growing up, but I was convinced I could do anything. My mother was very creative too; she had a beautiful garden. And my parents never put up any serious objections, like, How are you going to live? They thought, she can look after herself, she's invincible. It was probably luck, too. And I could draw, I could always draw. Just copying things.

I'm very driven. Not that I'm driving towards point A, I'm just driving. Getting known isn't the driving force – but I wouldn't want to be *not* known either. I like people writing about my work. Critics set you in context and it gives you back a sense of yourself, situates you. I've no interest in working blind, like a mole, just spitting out work. I think it's important to be known. Though being known can be hard because you're up for hatred as well as love!

I don't like being solitary, I always have loads of company, and I'm more likely to be in a relationship than not. I like having fun, partying, you know. Of course I'm on my own when I work. For some years now I've lived and worked in the same place. I do some teaching – which isn't really related to making art. I like a little bit of teaching – you're talking, it's company. Work is a strange state: it's not that I feel happy when I work, more like, time doesn't exist. That's happy. Because you're unconscious. Not like sleep. You can see and feel in lots of dimensions. Things I make are either really small or really big, there's no medium.

This picture here is about growing bigger and smaller. People think my pictures are conceptual but actually they're almost experiential. I didn't decide a mountain for this picture, I had no idea what I was going to do. I just put on a ground, and then I did the mountain. From a distance you see a mountain, and then maybe you spot the puff of smoke at the top, then you come closer and you see the little girl with a fire next to her. When I put the little figure on the top I got a fright because I thought she looked so lonely, so I put the fire on to keep her company – it's a nice puff of smoke, like she's sending up signals or something. She's very happy up there, the way she's lying, she's very relaxed. I've been painting little girls for a long time, but these are positively miniature! It's not like I'm trying to disappear, though. These creatures are absolutely huge to me, if you can imagine that. Would I like to be on the mountain like that? I think I am there.

Pat Liddy is a water-diviner, beekeeper and retired farmer. One trouser leg is clipped back ready for the bike. He lives in County Clare, in the house where he was born. His mother was there too till she went to live with his sister in Whitegate. There are about fifteen clocks in the room, cuckoo, rollerball and wall-wagger. An old valve radio is plastered into one wall.

That's my magic

Most of the clocks came from Germany. There was one fella came here looking for a spring. He fell in love with a sheepdog pup I had in the yard. So I gave it to him and then he came back and gave me a clock. After that people kept bringing clocks when I found them springs. Finding springs. That's my magic. You're not supposed to charge for finding a spring for people because it's a natural gift.

I don't think my father had the gift, but he died before I knew I had it. It's not something you can learn at school. When I left school I hardly knew how to read the paper. There was a teacher by the name of Miss Hawkins, but she was wicked. She gave me such a beating down the head that when I got home and opened my mouth it hurt my ears.

I've good hands. Anything I see done I could nearly do it after that. Most things about the place I've done myself. Or haven't done because I didn't have the price of it. I worked the farm all the time, doing everything that was ever to be done, train horses, plough, cut hay, cut turf. I could make any sort of cock of hay. When I was young I done everything. I ferreted rabbits. A shilling apiece. Did you ever see a ferret? You got into the pictures for a shilling. And maybe have a smoke as well. That time people would live only for the local shop being so obliging and giving them credit for a month or two. I don't think people are happier now they've got more money.

I did work hard. And my parents worked harder. If you had the weather you had to avail of it. Your biggest delight was after a day's work if you had a field of hay all stacked and it rained that night. You slept very happy.

I rent the farm out now. But I stay here, I live away, keeping going nice and gentle. I cook on the fireplace. I boil the kettle over the fire. Cook my eggs in a pea tin. I have an old gas cooker but I never use it. I haven't got a car. I never liked driving. I have a tractor but I don't like driving on the road. In a tractor you hear nothing. In a bicycle you hear everything. The furthest I ever went was Dublin. I went to an all-Ireland football final in 1963. I didn't like Dublin at all. I couldn't sleep at all with the traffic, the noise. Killarney was the furthest south I ever went. My sister and her husband are trying to bring me to England for the last twenty years. I'd go the odd time to Limerick, for a hurling match, or something I couldn't get in Tulla. I'm not a big shopper. If something's a bit worn I'd rather leave it as it is. Young people today are born with money. They know nothing else. They wouldn't know how to hang a kettle.

I've got the TV though. Since they came out. I like *Coronation Street*. 'Tis very funny. I like a good yarn, an insulting answer. *Coronation Street* is like Tulla. I go into Tulla three or four times a week. I go to a ballad session maybe Wednesday night. And I like a good conversation. There are some characters there. You wouldn't need to write a script. Their answers are fantastic. I used to go to films, then I saw a film being made when I was in Dublin that time, and I never went to a film after that. All the crews, all the cameras and the equipment out on the street. You saw what you'd see on the screen but you saw the back of it, behind the scene. It's a bluff job, sure.

I heard an old guy say one time you should always walk agin' the people. If a hundred people are walking that way and you didn't like it, you walk the other way.

Would you mind if I watch *Coronation Street* now?

pat liddy

*The Duffys, Carmel, Pete and their nine children,
live in County Meath. They have horses and hens.
Carmel taught the children to read and write and
decided not to send them to school.*

Home life

Pete

Hard to say what set us off in the direction we took. When Siobhán was
very small, and we were living in my mother's home, about three miles
from here, nothing seemed to fit with our way of thinking – though we
didn't know what our way of thinking was at the time. I remember, I was
working in Cork, diamond-drilling. I was always under pressure. It seemed
to be a policy of the company that people from around Dublin were being
shipped to Cork or Belfast, and vice versa. So, Siobhán was only about five
months old, and she didn't know me when I came home Saturday night.
Then I was off Monday morning, five o'clock. I knew this wasn't the way
I wanted to live. By the time Diane was born, actually the day Diane was
born, I just said, No, I'm out of here. So by the time Diane and Carmel
were out of the hospital I was out of a job.

I went down to the mines in Navan, and got a job there. And then
there were a series of strikes. So I bought a tractor and trailer and chain-
saw, bought in a couple of woods, cut them up and sold them for timber.
It was working out so well – not financially – but it was so marvellous to
be home and have the kids. I could throw the kids in the truck and bring
them round with me. And I thought, this is what life should be like.

My father died when I was three. He had an accident with a horse
when he was thirty-two, and lost his leg. He died of peritonitis in Navan

hospital. I was the youngest of four. My mother had to go back to work as a nurse. The only person who spent a great deal of time with me was my grandfather, who was a really marvellous horseman, really a genius. He was a judge of horses, he had a magic pair of hands and a very gentle nature, he was a lovely man. My mother came from the upper classes and she felt she had married beneath herself; he was merely a farmer's son. She never talked about him after he died. She drove a wedge between herself and myself, because I idolized my father the little that I knew him. I had marvellous time for my mother, I was one of her greatest admirers, but I really didn't like her very much. She was an incredible woman, she'd a strength that was scary. She went through really really bad times, horrendous times.

Carmel

When I was young, mothers were at home. I was born in '57. My mother wasn't a great house person. She couldn't really cope with the housework and the family and all that sort of stuff, but my father was unusual. He was a vet, and spent a great deal of time in the country, and I used to go with him. I was interested in it, and I realize now I learned a lot about animals and nature. My mother was a real townie. She thought if a thing could come out of a packet it was much better. My mother didn't have great health, and my father would have looked after us a great deal. He always tried to finish work early so he could pick us up from school and bring us in the car out the country somewhere, to a field, or up a lane, and he'd help us with the homework and play football with us maybe. He'd keep us out till teatime and then bring us home to my mother. He would bathe us; he had much more contact with us than the fathers of other children we knew.

He was very intelligent, and educated, but if you had an MA and I had a doctorate, he'd be terrified. He wouldn't really associate with his peers on a social level, saying they were all a pack of hypocrites. He hated posing, and airs and graces. He'd a great appreciation of farmers. He'd sit down by the fire with them and talk, and going home he'd say things like, Oh didja ever see how snug they are, and what a grand apple tart they had for their tea. So I was getting an appreciation of the country, and of simplicity. The one thing he couldn't understand was when I'd say to him that maybe some of the cleverest people were out digging spuds, they never bothered getting degrees. He just couldn't swallow that one at all. Academic success was very important to him. There were ninety-eight fellas when he was studying to be a vet, and one woman, and he said, By god she was some woman. I was the only girl in the family – I have five brothers – so he did encourage me to study, and do well at school. I had a great advantage from that point of view. In those days girls wouldn't have been much encouraged. As a family we were quite eccentric, and I think that's been a great help. It's easier not to worry too much about people laughing at you or sneering at you.

All the time people say to you, It's mad what's going on, the rat race. But everybody's running so fast they haven't time to think about it, so they keep doing it. The people who've done different, their approach is, Well, it's mad, so we'll stop doing it, and then we'll worry about what else we can do, we'll work it out as we go along. That's what makes people different, that they don't keep running after the person in front of them.

Pete

The toughest part is that society, starting with your neighbours, your friends, your relatives – who are the harshest judges of all – really put the screws to you. To withstand the pressure from your own is definitely the toughest. There's times I certainly felt quite beaten down by it and very isolated. Just two of us sitting out on the limb of a big tree, with somebody with a saw at the other end of the branch. When you stood back and looked, you could see the strategy: they'd take a run at you and give you a few wallops, and then go back and regroup. It was like that for many years. My eldest brother was the only one who thought what we were doing was marvellous. But bit by bit they came round. The change that came was as the children started to travel and be ambassadors for the family. They could handle themselves very well, none of them are intimidated in the least by adults, the smallest fellas will converse with you, because that's the way it's always been. The children are very gentle, and they're terrible loving to their animals – and still, we've reared pigs, beef cattle, sheep, chickens, and when the time comes for to feed us for the winter, I've seen the kids go to give the pig a scratch on the back before I shot it, saying, Well, this is the time, this is how life is.

home life

Carmel

People are saying there must be method in our madness somehow, because they're growing up to be decent people, sensible, responsible, not crazy, you can trust them to do a job.

Pete

People feared the children would turn out to be oddballs, that they wouldn't be able to socialize at all. Socialize is a big word. The boys all play hurling, and football, and they all love to hunt, which is very big in this county, and brings a lot of socializing. And of course there's a lot of them.

Carmel

Another thing that's very important is that we're both from within five miles of here, so we know people here. It's not like people who come from other countries, or from Dublin, to live in the country. In ways, knowing people here has made it harder. You can get away with a certain amount of deviant behaviour when you're a foreigner. People will say to you, We went to school with you, why can't you be like the rest of us? And on the other hand, they know if they lend you their trailer you'll bring it back.

I have a philosophy that what you need to get by is nothing. It's nice to have a bit of jam or go to the pictures, or do something extra, but as long as you have the basics, enough to eat, good food, a warm place to sleep, you get by. We've plenty of luxuries. We produce as much of what we eat as we can. We do without quite a lot.

Pete

People will not do without. Will not. Whatever it takes to get it, you must *have*.

Carmel

I was listening to the radio last week and some woman was talking about dogs in Germany, and how there weren't any pounds, no stray dogs and no dogs put down. There's such a high standard of living, she said, that eventually it filters down to the dogs! It'll get like that here if you wait long enough.

To some extent, we live quite well, by virtue of the fact that every-

carmel & pete duffy

body else is so rich. You'd want to see some of the black bags of clothes that come in here. We don't have to wear poor-quality clothes. They might be old, but they're good. We get a lot of shoes, school books. Even food. If there's something on in the parish and there's sandwiches left over, they send them up here. If we don't eat them the chickens will.

Pete

The compost bin is the last stop on the line, so nothing goes to waste. With the children we lay our political beliefs on the table. The idea of greed, or wanting more than your share, really is abhorrent to us. When you want way more than your share, there can be no end to what you want. You might justify yourself by saying, I work so hard I'm entitled to have a holiday house, and this might sound all right in words, but nobody works that hard, nobody works harder than we work. And we're not doing it to own an extra house. We discuss this at length with the children, we try to give them a clear picture of where we're at.

Carmel

I remember when I was at school there was a book called *Economic Geography*, about different people in different parts of the world. There was one thing that kept coming up, they'd say that people were subsistence farmers, they eke out a living growing a few bananas. The lowest place you could be was subsistence farming. My understanding of subsistence farming is that you produce what you need yourself, as far as you can, and if you have a surplus you can trade it for what you can't produce, or for luxuries. That's the way most of humanity has lived for most of the history of the world. The era we're now living in, which thankfully I think is drawing to a close, is actually an aberration. We think it's always been like that, but it's only been like that for a couple of hundred years in certain parts of the world.

One day last week they were saying the reason house prices were so high was there was a shortage of houses. How can there be a shortage of houses? Everywhere you look there's houses going up. Everybody wants to live in Dublin because they perceive that there's money. There's a hundred thousand people in Tallaght, and half of them are sitting at home going bananas twiddling their thumbs and walking the dog, you know. It's mad. I know this rural resettlement is catching on, but it's very small.

home life

In 1971 when we went into the EC, I remember thinking, what's all this EC, what's it about, and they were showing us films at school about the farmers in Holland and Denmark – they polish their pigs, they said, they scrub them with soap, there's no such thing as a small farmer, they all have six hundred pigs blah blah blah. Not like here where there's twenty-acre farms, forty-acre farms. If our farms all have to get bigger, what's going to happen to the little farms that get swallowed up? We lost ten or twenty thousand farmers in twenty years, and where are they now? They're either pulling pints in New York or London, or living in Tallaght on the dole. I don't think we're any better off. A few people are better off, and the economy is better, but life is worse.

It wasn't a definite decision in the beginning not to send the children to school. I was at home, and Pete was out at work all the time, and his mother was in the house. She was really nice with the children. When Siobhán was about three and a half and Diane was two and a half I taught the two of them to read. It was just something to do. I used the Ladybird keywords reading scheme because that was available in Trim. In a few months the two of them were reading quite fluently. So then I got them books that had simple texts they could read. I couldn't understand the whole big mystique about teaching children to read. When you can read you can read and what you need is practice, and books that you're interested in reading. If you want to know what it's about you'll look up the words or you'll ask your mother. Once they could read we just bought them books they were interested in. We taught them to write using the same Ladybird thing.

When Siobhán was four they announced at Mass that spring that if you wanted your child to go to school that September you should put your name down. So I put her name down, and when I went in, I said to the head nun, The two older children can read, so would you consider putting Siobhán into senior infants and Diane into junior infants? But the nun said, Oh no, if a child has never been to school before, it doesn't matter what they know, they have to start in first class. And then she told me there'd be four classes of forty children in that school that year, and I thought, however good the teachers are, what chance has one out of a hundred and sixty? So September came and went, and they were happy at home, they weren't bored, I could see they were learning things, little things appropriate to their age. I wasn't in a hurry to get them out of the house. I had more little ones anyway. And I couldn't afford to send them all to school, with the uniforms and the books.

I was happy at school myself. I was a good student, I was interested and I did very well. I was still a student when we got married. I was studying for my MA, which I didn't finish.

Pete

She was a star student. The nuns still have her essays from when she was eleven and twelve! I despise school. I really hated school. I went very little. I was a good student, I had no problem, but I didn't like it, I never seemed to fit in. I lived my day just to get home to the farm. I just fired the school-bag in the door and I was out again. So I was a hundred per cent behind keeping the children as far away from school as I could.

I emigrated to the United States when I was fairly young, and it was a great leveller for me. I spent fifteen years there. During that time I worked at high management level and nobody ever asked me could I write my name, not once. The Yanks' attitude was, Deliver, and you've got the job, and I delivered, and I got the job. I had no certificates. The most successful people in the business line were uneducated.

Carmel

Out of the people I've known in my life who have been schooly people, I've seen very very few who are able to process their education. Usually people are processed by their education.

Education is a confidence trick. You're in the baby room and they're all bigger than you, they all know more and you're nothing. And you slog your way up to sixth class, and then, wham, you're in first year in secondary and you're at the bottom of the pile again. Then you go to university, you're in a much bigger pool, and there's several really good brains like yours from a hundred schools like yours, and there are all these professors and doctors and this one and that one. An awful lot of it is to intimidate you – half the time they don't know beef from a bull's foot, they've got the job, they've got the bit of paper rolled up under their arm, they wrote some thesis. If you put them into a room and said, Here, get this room decorated, and gave them a bucket of paint, they wouldn't know where to start.

home life

Free education in secondary was brought in for everybody in 1966; before that it was fee-paying schools. So when I was at school, a whole lot of the children who were sent to secondary school, their parents wouldn't have been to secondary school – if one person in the family wanted to be something, they took education, and the others would have had to go out to work to support them. And so education was seen to be precious and desirable and difficult to get, and the gateway to wealth and prestige. It was, because very few people had it, but of course when everybody has it, it can't be, because everybody can't have wealth and prestige, it just isn't there for everybody. So they have to invent other ways of limiting the prestige and wealth and status.

I've heard of people who did unusual theses, like the architecture student who was going to do a project on Dara Molloy's new house, which had no septic tank, no toilet. He was told, Oh no, they wouldn't accept that as a project, it was too unusual, they'd have nothing to compare it to. They couldn't just look at it and see if the guy knew what he was talking about. It would have to be judged by the others. You can see that a certain amount of that is inevitable, but if he's supposed to be doctor-professor X, surely to God they can make their mind up about whether it's a piece of rubbish or the guy knows what he's talking about.

The next thing is: it used to be the case when I was in college that you could do an MA by major thesis or by minor thesis and exam. Well, since then it's become more and more that they don't want you to do a major thesis. They want everyone to sit the exam, they want to control: we'll just shout the stuff, you just regurgitate it back. The thesis is just a minor event. We don't want you going off for two years, doing your own thing and coming back with something this thick that we can't understand. It's coming to that with doctorates even. So by the time you are old enough that whatever you have to say might be listened to, you're totally pulped from all this marshalling, you haven't an original idea in your head, you're just past it, you're a fossil and a fogey. So I don't see the point of the whole thing at all except that you want to get a bit of paper and a slot and a salary.

An awful lot of that too is the extension of childhood, making longer and longer the period when the child is dependent and has to be looked after. You're too fecking old when you're in your thirties to be having your first child. I know myself. I could see my own insecurities and worries

about life getting bigger as I got older. They're putting off the responsibil-
ities of life longer and longer. Everything is theoretical and laboratory, it's
a thesis, it's a theory, you write it up and you prove it statistically. But if
you have to deal with a child that's crying, it's a real situation and you have
to deal with it. You can have fun, too, when you're bringing up a family.
You can have a laugh.

People seem to forget that universal education has only been invented in the last 250 years, and that doesn't mean people knew nothing before
that. They had different ways of passing on the wisdom, the culture of the
group. Universal education takes the weight off the culture to transmit the
wisdom and the knowledge, and maybe that's destructive to the culture. If
you're not going to use the universal education system, you're going to have
to hope that the culture in this family, and the extended family, and the
neighbours, is rich enough to prepare the children for living. Because that's
really what it's about when all's said and done.

home life

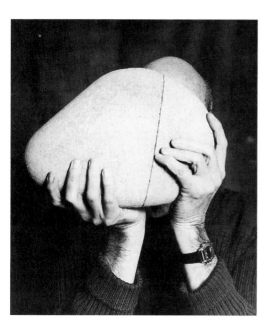

Tim Robinson has walked, mapped and written about the Aran Islands, the Burren and Connemara. He runs Folding Landscapes from Roundstone in Connemara.

Beyond

I've told the story of how I came to be in Ireland so often that I remember the story but can't remember the facts ...

I always wanted to study science and maths and I always wanted to be a painter. At the same time. I really believed that if you wanted to be a painter you should do it entirely by yourself, that art education was mere interference with aesthetic minors. But I knew I couldn't do mathematics by myself, so I went to Cambridge to study it. Actually I was going to do physics, but in theoretical physics the first-year course was pure and applied mathematics, and I enjoyed that so much I stuck with the mathematics, and taught mathematics and physics to kids in Turkey for a few years afterwards. These were mainly Turkish students who were studying to go into a college which is now called University of the Bosphorus, which sounds wonderfully romantic. We lived on the shores of the Bosphorus, on a steep lane called the Street of the Lantern-lit Tomb from the tomb of an old Dervish master on the hillside above. Nearby was where Medea spread poison on the shore, in the legend of the Argonauts, and where St Simeon Stylites sat on top of a pillar for years. So it was romantic, indeed.

Then I gave up teaching and decided to paint full time. We moved from Turkey to Vienna, as I thought that was probably a quiet European backwater for my early efforts. I had a couple of exhibitions in Vienna, of rather surreal and horrible paintings. I was probably influenced by the creepy, cold-war atmosphere of Vienna. This would have been in the very early sixties, and it was a hallucinatory city to live in. No one talked about what they had done or even where they had been over the last twenty or thirty years, under the Nazis and then the Russians. One day we were walking around the Ringstrasse, we passed a door that said International Artists' Club, and they welcomed us with open arms, told us we were members and that we were going to meet there, for wine and conversation, and it was all very pleasant. We were wondering how all this was funded, because we hadn't been asked to pay very much. Later on we heard that it was funded by the CIA through the Ford Foundation, to encourage artists to defect from Hungary. In Vienna artists were always forming little clubs and movements and secessions, and every time two of them sat down, two more people would materialize, the spy from the west and the spy from the east. So the most minuscule groups ended up largely composed of spies.

After three years there we came back to England and I did what young up-and-coming painters do in England. I exhibited at the John Moores Biennale and was picked up by a London gallery, Signals, which was the avant-garde gallery at the time, and had exhibitions there, and then at the Lisson Gallery, which has since become very famous. Then I started doing big environmental installations, and got into psychological difficulties with all that. The arts world was becoming more and more like show-biz, and getting money for these big constructions was a matter of selling an idea before you knew it existed. As I have always believed in working beyond your known capabilities, I've never been any good at selling ideas to people – and hated the thought of doing so. I've never been any good at any art form that involved co-operation; I don't have the sort of personality that can make the same demands on others as I do on myself. I've always been aware of the necessity to wait for things to happen in myself and you can't do that if other people are waiting for you or upon you.

So I began to do smaller and smaller and more and more personal, hidden work that only a few visitors to my studio ever saw. And I also began to write, and enjoyed that. I liked shutting my notebook and the day's work being absolutely invisible at the end of the day.

I'd gone on a hitchhiking holiday around Norway, to the Lofoten Islands to see the midnight sun – I was already working in terms of landscape and compass directions. I've always enjoyed being by myself, particularly in the countryside. And when I came back I said to M, We must go to Norway. But while I'd been away she'd seen the film *Man of Aran,* so we went to Aran instead, to see if it was as good as the film. We spent about ten days there, and it was nothing like the film, though it was very, very beautiful, and it re-awoke a childhood interest in natural history – the flowers were absolutely wonderful. We must have been there in June. Then later that year, for various reasons to do with landlords, rents, the usual London hassle, we had to move out of our flat and decided to take this mighty leap into the unknown. I wanted a place in which to work absolutely privately, to retire from the scene, to experiment, and find out where I was going, and Aran seemed perfect for that.

When we went to the Aran Islands, I had begun to write an experimental novel, though I didn't get very far with that. I was spending all my time exploring the island, and beginning to pick up a bit of Irish, and collect placenames, even before I had any Irish, which was absurd. I spent a lot of my time walking, botanizing, beginning to learn about geology and archaeology, and finding it fascinating from so many points of view.

Then one day the postmistress said, Oh Tim, why don't you make a map of the islands? – and I thought that was a marvellous idea. I started that night, not knowing anything about maps. Except that maps had actually been an interesting metaphor for me. I'd done a lot of drawings of map faces, little pen drawings, which were half like portraits and half like maps. Unfortunately some of those damned Viennese surrealists stole the best of them. And the abstract works I did in London had to do with direction and sensations of walking through a landscape, towards the sun for instance, or across a pass. Ideas about significant topographical steps, but at a very abstract level. So trying to make a real map seemed to me a wonderful way of putting together all the different sorts of layers of information I was beginning to accumulate about Aran, and maybe expressing something about the place.

In fact I was trying to reinvent mapping, so that it would be an expressive art, as well as being true to fact. I think that's also a structural principle in my writing. I'm trying to use an enormous burden of fact as a formal constraint, just as somebody else might choose to use a very difficult, elaborate rhyme scheme or metre to create a continuous necessity for invention. It pleases me very much that in my book on Aran I have worked

45

beyond

in a mention of every species of butterfly recorded on Aran; it's absurd, but it took some ingenuity and suggested connections of thought I wouldn't otherwise have hit on.

When I'd published the Aran map, I happened to read something about the Burren in County Clare, just a phrase from Praeger that caught my fancy, so I went and had a look at that, and couldn't really get a feel of the place. Then one day, about the beginning of November, we were walking across the hills towards Ballyvaughan, a sunny autumn day, and as we climbed up the pass we heard dogs barking and men shouting. A huge herd of cattle were being driven up the track – because in the Burren it's the opposite way round to what they do in other parts of Europe: they take the cattle up on the high limestone crags at the beginning of winter, and bring them down at the beginning of summer. The two dates on which they do this correspond to the two main festivals of the Celtic year, which divide the year into the two Celtic seasons of winter and summer. And this happened to be one of those days on which the life of the Burren hinges. It was marvellous to see it happening, to hear it all echoing on that still afternoon. That gave me a feeling for the place. And I felt that the Burren was like a fruit on the branch waiting to be plucked.

So I spent two years doing a map of the Burren. I was usually doing the fieldwork in the autumn or spring. A lot of that was a very lonely and harsh experience. Cycling around, staying in chilly bed & breakfasts, and spending long days out by myself, nobody really knowing who I was or what I was doing, frequently in wind and rain, waiting for days for rain to let up. Then I did another map of the Aran Islands because the first one was a very crude affair. By that time I was in a good relationship with all the scientists and specialists who came to these areas, and was picking up a vast amount of information from them, and beginning to work on a map of south Connemara, which is incredibly complex. I decided to do this walk along the south coast of Connemara, which must have taken a total of months. I did it in pieces; I have actually walked all the way along this amazingly zig-zag coast, an absolutely crazy thing to do and I don't know how I did it, but it forced me to visit all sorts of desolate corners I'd not have seen otherwise, and I made a few exciting finds that way, of rare plants, or archaeological sites.

When I began that walk I didn't know anything about fractals, which had been invented after I'd left the mathematical scene, and it was actually a literary critic who first sent me an article on fractals, and I looked into them, and of course I found a close relationship with some things I had done at Cambridge under Professor Besicovitch, which had seemed very bizarre and almost pointless at that stage, and now have turned out to be absolutely crucial, seminal. Here was an exciting new way of understanding natural forms like coastlines, cloud shapes, the outlines of trees, that had always intrigued me. And just recently, because I haven't been able to write anything, I've gone back to mathematics, and been reading about fractals in more detail, trying to follow through some of the calculations. It's wonderful stuff, revelatory, the potentialities of abstract forms.

I do believe in obsessiveness as a source of creative thinking, as a source of art. I find that the only way I can write about anything is to cultivate an obsession with it. To get beyond conventional responses, by physically experiencing it, by dwelling on it mentally until something breaks and images and ideas begin to come through.

I've always been particularly interested in spaces of various sorts, including the abstract ones. And then the paintings, which were abstract, and then later on the actual maps, these are all dealings with space. We are spatial objects – which to most people would seem the lowest possible level of being, but it isn't to me, it's extraordinarily important. If you start to explore any space either conceptually or physically, you begin to find out that spaces are bigger on the inside than they are on the outside. Labyrinths are an obsession with space.

Recently I have remembered one or two little incidents from very early days which are about space. I remember when I was about eight thinking about a sequence of roads that went past the primary school I went to, and wondering would they link up with other roads I knew of lying in another direction. I went off an expedition on my bike to check this out, and lo and behold if you cycled far enough you could come back by these other, less familiar roads. I can remember the shapes of them, their map, still.

Then I became very interested in perspective. I remember learning that parallel lines met at infinity, and so I thought if parallel lines meet at infinity, anything else could happen at infinity. You could make drawings of infinity, with lots of parallel lines meeting dramatically, and then add anything else that you could draw. I liked drawing elephants, so I drew lots

beyond

of elephants at infinity. Once I tried to explain to some friends of mine that things farther away looked smaller; I drew a picture of a road going away over hills and getting smaller, and showing it to one of these kids who said, But that's ridiculous. I could see it clearly, but they couldn't. So I had some sort of affinity for space.

But the maps were a complete chance, even a mistake, a distraction and dispersion of life's way, I sometimes think. I'm not interested in doing other maps. I've done my ABC, Aran, Burren and Connemara. People are always suggesting I come and do Donegal, and so on. I could just go on, and quite profitably if it weren't for the fact that each map takes so many years, but I'll not make any more maps unless I have some radical new ideas about what maps are about. At the same time, maps are what we live on. Folding Landscapes, which is the business side – a financial damage-limitation exercise – it publishes and distributes the maps. Fees from talks and royalties from the books are pretty limited. We've had some strokes of luck, we have our own lovely house on the seashore here in Roundstone, but we also live carefully and at a low income level – we don't have a car, for instance – and so the maps bring in enough.

Some of the people in the village are interested in what we do, and of course I've been pestering all of them about placenames and so forth. In the Irish-speaking areas there's an immense interest in the naming of things and people. People were fascinated by what I was doing in Aran, and in Connemara as well. I started to write a series of articles for the *Connacht Tribune* when I was doing the Connemara map. I went through townland by townland, talking about the placenames I found and the stories connected with them, and the archaeological sites and folklore, asking people to contact me with further information. This was very productive. I was amazed at the degree of penetration into the glens of Connemara that the *Connacht Tribune* has. They go into the most remote places. I used to knock on a door, anywhere, in the remotest corners, and they'd say, Oh, you're the man from Roundstone! Or the woman of the house would say, Himself has been waiting for you, there's a rock he wants to show you. People were waiting for me to come, and were annoyed that I hadn't; their placenames were on the tips of their tongues for me: That is Cnoc something; that's Glenn na whatsit.

The big work I've done in these years is *Stones of Aran*. It's a literary construction, despite its factual overload. It doesn't matter whether the

Aran Islands exist or not; if I had had the capacity to imagine it all, that would have been equally good. It's a very highly shaped book, not just the sentences and paragraphs, but the book as a whole has an architecture to it, it's a very closed structure. And I don't want to write a *Stones of Connemara*. Or a *Stones of Provence*.

At the moment I'm doing a computerized archive of all the place-names I've collected – about six thousand – with a lot of information on each. I find an interest in that kind of work. I like pedantry, I like getting things right, and finding cross-connections between names and people. I'm ridding myself of more facts than anyone probably knew there were about Connemara. Getting them off my back. Ridiculous bits of information I've carried around in my head for years that nobody else knows about or cares about or ever will. I have to guard this archive. Nonsense! That's the obsessive bit, and now I'm discharging it onto the computer which can groan under it.

I have been trying for some time to write in a completely different way, and invent for myself a new style. I've written a few pages, the beginning of a book on Connemara, which reads like the end of a book on Connemara, they're so violent and abrupt and extreme. So I'm just having to wait and hope that something will come out of that. It's a difficult time, though. You feel not only that you won't be able to write anything in the future but also that you never have written anything in the past.

Personal names. Yes. I did my paintings and my environmental constructions under the name Timothy Drever. Drever was my mother's maiden name – she was Scottish – and I like the name very much. Also, just at the time I left Cambridge and started to do some painting, there seemed to be someone called Robinson around who was doing art criticism. Never heard of him since. Robinson was my father's name. Later on when we went to the Aran Islands it seemed too complicated to have two names. It was bad enough having just one non-island name. The reasons for changing the name seemed to be fairly trivial, but I suppose underneath that there was some significance in it. Changing a name is like shedding skins. I have another name, *Fear na mapai*, given to me by the Aran Islanders, it means man of the maps. I'm very proud of that name – though ultimately I don't want to be remembered for my maps.

beyond

50

Willie Kingston, with his wife Patricia, has fenced off twenty acres from his dairy farm and planted trees, dug lakes, introduced birds and animals, living and crafted, and created a sanctuary to which wildlife gravitates. Model fishermen stand in the lake and a concrete salmon leaps between real ducks, geese and swans. Moorhens zip between fibreglass waders. A real hare jumps over a model rabbit.

All of creation

The two best things I ever did were stopping going to church and making this. There would be endless hours gone into it, but I'd've given that a million times for what I've got out of it, because every time I go down there, there might be a clutch of baby ducks or moorhens, rabbits, baby hares.

The whole thing is going back to when I was very young. I always had a great love of all of creation, of every human thing, from the tiniest plant. I grew up here on the farm and I learned that you can't take something from the land without giving something back, or you'll be punished for it. I think everybody should leave bits and pieces for trees and for wildlife, wildflowers, all of creation.

The bigger farmers now, they'll remove everything, they'll have huge herds of cows and they get themselves into a rut of life that they'll never ever get out of. It won't be a question of not having enough, all their problems will come from having too much. They're punished from every angle, they don't have time to see all the beauties around them. It's as if their minds are computerized just to see grass and cows and milk, and 'tis all to make money which they don't need at all – or they need very very little of it. We're the only species that uses money. All the other species get on fine without it.

There is too much milk there at the moment. There are new regulations that milk has to be at a certain cell count. If you don't get your milk right it's not going to be taken, you'll have to pull out the stopper and drain it all out – though the milk is absolutely perfect, you'd give it to your nearest and dearest. The only reason for removing the milk is that there are lakes of it there and it's one way of reducing it, and one way of the creameries getting rid of the smaller suppliers. It's a lot easier to collect the milk from the bigger farms. You can get the same amount of milk from one big farm as from twenty small ones. And these big farms have the buying power, they have the machines to destroy, to drain, to remove ditches to create one huge square of ground without a tree, without a butterfly, without a rabbit, without a bird in it.

The only way I can do something about it is to do something myself, and I'm delighted that I was in a position to do that, to give back to creation all that creation gave me and be part of it. We are all part of the whole universe, one way or another, and it's part of us. Even a high windy day now, it affects every living thing. The trees hate it, the whole atmosphere is disturbed, even your own mind is not as relaxed as it would be on a calm day.

Close to the house there was an old spring we used when I was very young, and it was still rising out of the ground. Then I thought one day that if that was dug out you could make a lake. So I did, and it turned out so well that we decided to dig out more of them. It wasn't long dug out, and on the little island in the centre, rushes grew, and in a very short time there was a moorhen's nest. That was the first feedback I got from what I had done.

There was nothing ever really planned, and I think that's why it turned out so well. You did one thing and then you saw something else to be done and you did that. And then it continued on and on. It would just come into your mind that a particular plant would complement another. You've a great mixture of wild areas, and areas that would be kept. But I always say that however much you do you'll never be able to do what nature will do itself. A river now, and a pathway, and mature trees, and bluebells, there'd be no garden you could create yourself that would be as peaceful or as pleasant or as natural.

It's difficult to describe what it has given me, but it's like a deepdown fulfilment, and constant feedback. If someone offered me fifty million, a billion pounds, I wouldn't part with it. There's no money would buy it. The pleasure it has given me has been the continuous work and seeing it come to fruition. We've never actually sat and enjoyed it! There's bunches of nettles to be pulled, and clipping to be done, grass-cutting, it's all there staring you in the face. Occasionally we just have to pick up our tail and head off. Or when someone comes we'll enjoy it with them. Like the wedding we're going to have in the church next month. We'll sit down on that day and enjoy it with them.

I've worked so hard since I was tiny. We were always reared up to the point that you rarely sit down, you've just got to keep working. My father worked all day and then into the night. He wouldn't be a man to give himself any pleasure. When he was dying he said to me, Don't work too hard. He was quite a religious man, so it would have been part of that. Religion wouldn't worry me at all. I can see God in all creation, but I wouldn't feel directly in touch with Him.

All the different areas I made, like the church and the beach, they all blend in together. There's a place for fun and crack, in the cottage. And the church would be a church where all human beings can feel more or less one. They can all keep their identity, Protestant, Catholic, Presbyterian, Jewish. And there's the wild area that the wild birds come to.

I started putting the figures and the creatures in at the same time as the rest. I'd see something I liked, creations of man that would add to the beauty of the place. I'd have an interest in art, and might go into a gallery when I was in town, but a lot of modern art – I just cannot see anything in it. To me it shows a mind that's completely confused and traumatized and wouldn't know at all where it would be going. A painting to me now would be say a Highland scene, with Highland cattle, completely natural.

I try to get the balance right, something that's so hard to do. You're either a workaholic or you do nothing. Being happy within oneself has to come from the inside out – appreciating the beauty that's all around you and not abusing it. Going back a short distance in our history, we hunted for our living. Some people still like fishing, shooting, hunting with dogs. That aggressiveness, or cruelty, is still in people. But I think it's leaving them with each generation. I think respect for the natural world is increasing. More people are understanding you'd need food and you'd need shelter and you'd need friends – and good health. If you have that you have it all.

all of creation

Two sisters and a brother farm forty acres by a reservoir on the river Lee. We had several picnics at the bottom of one of their fields, by the lake. We watched them getting in the cows, they saw our canoe.

We're Regans

We're Regans, *says Johnny,* we're here all our lives. Me, and Mary, she's the eldest, and Sheila, she's the youngest. 'Twas our grandmother as got the farm; they were Halls. No, we've none of us been out of the country.

There's always the cows, *says Sheila,* there's always work to be done when you've cows, you've sheep and you've tiny turkeys. There's no call for describing whether it's quiet or dull or powerful here.

The farm is so clean it's like a child's painting: the house, the front yard, the back yard, the milking sheds, the hay barns are painted green and red and white, and the gates are silver.

Every other year we paint and whitewash. It's not so often, really, *says Sheila, giving the range of house and buildings a half-nod sideways.* Every day we sweep the yard. I do the back and Mary does the front. The milking sheds we whitewash every year. Mary does the top one, Johnny the middle one, and I do the end one. Each of us has an old pan to measure the ration. We do five cows at a time. Then there's the yard to be swept again. We have twenty cows and a few sheep, a sheepdog called Shep, a runful of turkeys – we don't fatten them too much, people like a tidy turkey nowadays. And there's three little girls from back the road who come every Saturday –

Every day, *Mary corrects.* They ride bikes and eat bonbons and help with the cows. On Saturdays we take them to mass.

The yard was concreted in the sixties, after the ESB dam was built and the valley flooded and they lost half their eighty acres. They had to think again, and dig a new well.

How long did it take to flood the valley? *Johnny is as excited as the day the flooding began.* The water came round every bush, every tree, then next day it made a mound an island with a tree, and the next day the tree was gone, and then houses were gone.

    Sheila remembers swimming in the swelling river. Every day in the summer, *she says.* Every day was the summer.

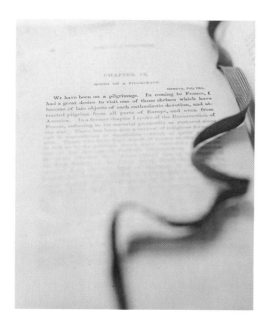

M lives as a solitary in a house that belongs to a neighbouring monastery. She earns a living by doing translations and assessments for drug companies. She works from home, but attends mass at the monastery; the monks also allow her to borrow books from their excellent library.

A convert from nothing

My first encounter with the Catholic Church was when I was a student in Scotland. A group of us went to a thirteenth-century priory which was being restored. It was a bit surreal, the beautiful monastic church had no roof. There was a fire – it was pretty cold at night. We arrived at the end of vespers, during the kyries, and I glimpsed something in the Gregorian melody: if you go deep enough, things connect and you're connected to everything that is.

When I entered monastic life a few years later I was a convert from nothing. I had been brought up to believe that the brave new world had answers to everything. Science and socialism would solve mankind's ancient ills. I wasn't convinced. I'd started a doctorate in pharmacology on the Continent, and I thought, this is a waste of time if I'm going into a monastery. I think from very early on I had a yen for more solitude, which to me meant more freedom and more radical separation. For several years in that community I had virtually no visitors from outside, so it was a pretty extreme version of going out into the desert. In the end it didn't work out, and I went to a semi-eremitical community in France. I was very happy there, but it was (a) too French, and (b) I'd come to realize that a community is still a community; you have an audience, and to me the solitary life is essentially that you haven't got an audience. I have an exhibitionist streak in me as well! I could have set up shop as some pseudo-spiritual sixties freak-out, but I had nothing to say!

I think being able to support yourself financially is very important. Traditionally the monastic orders did always earn a good secular living – they farmed, they brewed; they didn't, until the late nineteenth century, make pious knick-knacks or live off mass stipends. Families probably always gave some money, but basically the monasteries earned their own money. I had to find a way of being solitary and earning a living. So things came together by accident. I left the French community and went to Paris. The first day I was there I wanted to shoot myself! I hadn't seen more than about nine people together for three years and I got off at the Gare d'Austerlitz at rush-hour! To some extent a modern city is ideal if you want to be solitary. And the French are good at leaving you alone. With my knowledge of pharmacology, I started doing technical translation and reporting for the drug industry. Then the electronic side of things got going – fax and so on – so it didn't really matter where you were, and I was able to come back to Ireland.

The monastic tradition has always included manual labour; it has always been technologically quite advanced, as well as plugging into the tradition of philosophy; and I think that balance – rather than the purely subjective piety of the more contemplative orders – is very healthy. From having worked in industry I know you cannot do more than about five hours a day at the computer and translating full pelt. The balance, then, to go out and dig the spuds, is very good. People tend to think that the monastic life consists of eighteen hours' ecstasy a day!

I don't think you could start here, in a cottage in the countryside; you have to journey to find it. When you enter a monastery it's seen as a prolongation of baptism, a death to what you were and a rising towards a new way of being. It's very painful, and I don't think there's any way round it. By trying to make it more human you're just prolonging it. There has to be an actual cutting off. But solitude – being a hermit or a recluse – is different. It's a deepening of what you've already learned. Not turning away from communion but going further in. T.S. Eliot's still point, I suppose.

Monasticism seems to me close to atheism. The monk is primarily the one who doesn't know, who is searching. Monasticism is not about religion as such, it's not a level of practice. A lot of people can relate to monasticism but not to the parish. The order I entered isn't a teaching order, I think that's important. They're not telling other people how to live. Many who are in religious orders feel they have a mandate to interfere in people's lives. One of the huge sins of the Catholic Church has been to stress the institution of marriage and ignore the quality of relationships. You could apply that to religious life as well. If someone's in there, they've got to stay in there; even if they're a square peg in a round hole and getting nowhere, no one would encourage them to leave. Maybe if they left they might come back and really live the life. A lot of people would gain from being chucked out, but most people are too frightened. One of the basic insights of Christianity is about love casting out fear. The institution tends to want to control people through fear. Silence, for example, meant you could have no opposition. Unfortunately, we end up wanting to be controlled. Silence should be about freedom, about going beyond words, beyond social pressure and conformism.

The essence of the solitary life isn't saying a lot of prayers, it's standing on your own two feet and taking responsibility for your own life, accepting what you've done and what you are. Most forms of life are constructed to prevent that. Christ said, Call no man on earth your father. So how come we've ended up with a church in which anyone who has any authority at all is addressed as Father? There's one father in heaven and he's His father and our father, and then suddenly there are all these spiritual fathers jumped up from somewhere – I've always read the Gospel with a feminist slant as 'those fellas bossing'! What it actually says is: YOU must call no one but me Father. The day I told my father I was becoming a Catholic (to him, that was joining the fascists – he'd been in Spain in the civil war and that was his first real encounter with the Catholic Church), he lowered *The Times* at breakfast and said: Now your father is in heaven so you won't need anything from ME!

I've always believed that power corrupts. I suppose I'm an anarchist. Apart from the sacramental food and mystery of life, the Church gives me a helpful intellectual framework and spiritual tradition. The power structures I reject. I'd rather not come to an open clash about it because at the moment if you push too hard the whole thing could keel over. When I see some of the odd sects coming along, and all the places you can go in the west of Ireland on retreat, I feel that for the Westerner, you're only compounding the problem by taking on – Buddhism, for example. The

a convert from nothing

Church shouldn't be about imposing submission and passivity. 'Father knows best' is as far from the Gospel as one can get, but still all too common in Catholic countries.

A friend of mine, a very bright computer person, said years ago that he felt he'd chosen freedom while I'd locked myself up in a hen coop. Twenty-five years on, we meet again. He's hardly to be pitied – very nice Georgian farmhouse – but he's got a mortgage and kids and relatively I'm the one who seems free now. Not having dependants helps, of course, but I'm lucky I've got a skill which is marketable and doesn't involve teamwork. Once you've got that, you're free, whereas the wings of high-fliers are pretty clipped, aren't they?

When I was working in the pharmaceutical industry, I said to some of the people there: I think you've got a kind of slave mentality; you do what you've been told to do even if you could do it better. I don't care if you're on £40,000 a year, you're still a slave. Even if you're washing the floor you can do it well or badly. Most people get revenge by doing a job badly, and that's terribly alienating. I have a nasty feeling that as soon as you set up something like a monastic community with a shared vision, or a family, this is what happens: everybody's playing a role and not being themselves. In most families I know, there's a lot of neurosis, and controlling, and bullying. And it's not always the one who's doing the beating up who's the villain of the piece!

If one really reads the Gospel, really lets it speak, it's pretty subversive. I don't know how the Church ever got to see herself as defender of the family, because if you read the Bible, all that Christ ever says about families is, leave them. He apparently didn't marry. The apostles had families, some of them, but they left them. I wonder how we ever got from there to calling everyone with any authority Father.

I oscillate between wishing I lived on an island like Skellig, and on the other hand being enthused by the idea of getting onto the World Wide Web. I went to a retreat place recently, which made me think that the ideal would be if a place like that had a link with chaplaincies in universities. People could come there to have a wider horizon for a while. I'm convinced that there is a treasure there. I do think it's iniquitous that students leaving a 'good Catholic school' – and even university – will have read some of the great minds in literature, but won't have read Augustine's *Confessions*. Their idea of religion is based on cut-down catechism that they quite rightly think they outgrew at thirteen. Friends involved in religious education tell me that in the present climate if you say anything remotely controversial, the parents, particularly the ones who never go to church, are there in the morning saying, What's this about never mind the Rosary? And, bang.

a convert from nothing

Séamas de Barra and Patrick Zuk recently moved to a tall house in Cork overlooking the river Lee. The most important feature of the house was that they could get two grand pianos up the stairs and play them without disturbing each other. Patrick is a composer and pianist, Séamas a composer and teacher. They have a houseful of books, and no telephone, television or radio.

A life in common

Séamas

If we want to know what people have to say, we turn to the minds that are in all these books. We don't turn on the television, or go out and buy the paper.

Patrick

There was never a choice for us to live as we do. It was absolute internal necessity. People choose to interpret the way we live our lives as an implied criticism of theirs.

Séamas

Sometimes you do stop and realize that other people don't feel or think or value the same things, and you say to yourself, am I out on a limb?

Patrick

When you tell people you don't have a television set, or a radio, or a telephone, or that you don't read newspapers, sometimes the reactions are very hostile. Reactions in Dublin to my not having a telephone were frankly disbelief, resentment. They thought I was selfish. I said, Well, it only takes a day for a postcard to get to Cork.

Séamas

We're quite willing to walk down to the station to make a telephone call, rather than have a telephone in the house. The thought that I finish my teaching and I can sit through an evening without being disturbed, without being invaded, is a blessing. If something is really that urgent the message will get through.

Patrick

To compose, you have to go down into yourself. To read a book, you have to earn it, there has to be an attempt to get down to bedrock.

Séamas

The mother of one of my students recently told me she objected to him reading books. She found him looking up words in a dictionary, and thought it was very peculiar altogether, as if I must have had some sort of abnormal influence over him that he would torture himself in this way even when I wasn't there! I find it profoundly disturbing that picking up a book or looking up a word in a dictionary should be considered a suspicious activity – one that might lead to thought? To independence?

Patrick

Maybe people object to reading because it looks as if you're not doing anything. So does composing. It's torture sometimes, trying to finish something. The last orchestral piece I wrote, I got into an absolute state about it, really worked up, almost to the point of paralysis.

Séamas

Some things come very easily, and some don't. Composing, like any artistic activity, if it's to be real at all, has to be process of self-discovery, and that's why it's much easier to write somebody else's music for them. I can come along and look at a piece by Patrick and put my finger on a fault. Or with my students, I can show them how it can go next. But I can't do that with my own things. I don't know what the notes should be until I have discovered that aspect of myself which they're defining.

Some composers have an extraordinary fluency, a direct link to their own consciousness, most notably Mozart; it just came out right all the time. On the other hand you have Beethoven, who hammered and bashed and rewrote and wrestled ideas into shape.

Patrick

And literally pounded the shite out of his piano when he was deaf, so badly that he actually wrecked it.

Our needs are very simple – a roof over our head, peace and quiet to work. We're very lucky that our lives are devoted to what we feel is essential, that we can discuss questions like: What are we? What are we the product of? What assumptions underlie the society of which we're a part? Where do these ideas come from? Reading and talking – with each other and with friends – provide the context for these questions.

Séamas

That student's mother I was talking about, she couldn't believe I had friends. She thought I must be completely anti-social. We're fortunate in having many and very dear friends – who would doubtless also be considered vastly eccentric. It's not necessarily that we always talk about Schopenhauer or Wagner, it's the chit-chat of a life in common. Patrick would have a far greater public profile than I would, with his concert activity, but we lead very retired lives altogether, out of circulation.

Patrick

When we're at home, we don't spend every hour of the day in each other's company. We've arranged the house in such a way that we can be completely separate. If Séamas is working, I might not see much of him for days at a time. But we always have dinner together, that's the one thing we always do. For the last couple of years, life has been quite disrupted – we've moved house, had builders in, and so on – but I used to get up at five o'clock in the morning before I started the day's work, even on days when I was going to Dublin, in order to read for an hour so that I felt set up for the day.

Séamas

We talk about things a lot, about things we've read; sometimes we have quite heated arguments. We might listen to the Beethoven quartets and have a systematic discussion of some aspect of them.

a life in common

Patrick

Discussing the Beethoven quartets might sound like a bizarre way to spend time to most people, but who would want to watch television when you can come into contact with a mind like Beethoven's? Don't tell me that people are criticizing or judging what they see on television. If they did, they wouldn't spend so much time in front of it. Often it seems that television, and most pop music, are designed to stop activity of any kind, any thinking. To a frightening degree I think people are in flight from themselves.

In colleges and universities the student is a consumer and a customer and has to be satisfied. They're wonderful and marvellous and any shite is fine – like mummy praising every bowel movement. An atmosphere where anything goes is not helpful to the person who does want to learn something. There's often a very real frustration that you're suffocating in a bog of superlatives.

What's frightening about the world we live in is the level of infantility, of self-gratification. There's no sense of serving something outside oneself, just satisfaction of the crudest instinctual drives – sexual, power over other people. People don't know what to do with the unbridled freedom they're offered. With the collapse of Christianity, there's nothing to orientate them. Hence this morbid clinging to material possessions, morbid clinging of children to parents and vice versa. In the culture we live in, you think your child is going to provide you with all the gratification you're entitled to have; and then the next minute you're telling the child she's good for nothing – after all the money you've spent, everything you've sacrificed.

People have so much uncertainty about living their lives. How many books are there about how to have a good relationship, how to be a good parent, how to be a good child, how to make friends and influence people? What are these books a sign of? People are cut off from their instincts for what's good for them.

Séamas

Patrick's sister was given a book called *Getting the Love that You Want and Keeping the Love that You Find*, or something like that.

Patrick

Getting the love that you *want.*

séamas de barra & patrick zuk   68

Séamas
It consisted of exercises you did with your partner.

Patrick
Self-actualizing exercises. Yes, dear. Can't wait.

Séamas
The final chapter was 'Seeking Professional Help'!

Patrick
People think that a relationship is going to give them everything, when there's so much you can only provide yourself. To what extent are people seen as things? Things that give things?

Séamas
I remember my father saying when I was sixteen or seventeen, What can I give you? I tried to explain to him that nothing that I really wanted could be given to me by anyone except me.

Patrick
It's so sad when you hear parents say, But we gave him everything. From the first bicycle onwards, there's an account to be kept and a very heavy price to pay, and that's subservience.

Séamas
We were both completely oblivious to any kind of youth culture. Looking back on it, I must have been quite a puzzle to my parents. My father was very sociable, and a sportsman, and I was completely impervious to his encouragements. I couldn't stand at all this running around a field after a ball. I remember being taken to a match to be indoctrinated into this world of team spirit, and I said I didn't understand why they didn't give each player a ball and they could score as many goals as they wanted. My father must have thought, Uh oh, here's somebody who's completely missed the point!

I spent most of my childhood quite solitary, painting – originally I wanted to be a painter. Within a week of discovering what music was at the age of fifteen, I was composing. I knew this was what I wanted to do.

Music grafts onto your personality. It immediately becomes part of your understanding of the world.

Patrick

There certainly wasn't any encouragement to study music. The headmaster of my school told me that music was an occupation for women and nancy-boys!

Séamas

The piano came into the house because my sister wanted to play. There was no music in the family. My sister gave up very quickly, and that summer I taught myself music, how to read, how to get around the keyboard.

Patrick

The big danger of music is that you have all these auto-erotic fantasies of appearing as soloist playing your concerto in front of crowds of thousands. It not only engages one's intellect and one's feelings, but there's also a physical, visceral response.

Séamas

As a mode of thinking, it's completely independent from and parallel to ordinary thinking. Most performers and music students never engage these questions at all, or look at how music works at a technical level.

Patrick

Teaching is the vile body, isn't it. If we both had the luxury of a private income, I'd compose and give half a dozen concerts a year.

Séamas

I would still teach, but I would choose my pupils carefully – people who had proved their interest and ability – and not do as many hours.

Patrick

Even though in an ideal world I wouldn't teach, or would only have one or two pupils, it has been a fascinating insight into our culture, our society, its rejection of a past, a context, a culture.

Séamas

Teaching has been valuable to me. Having to rethink the teaching of technical matter has sharpened my understanding of it. You can see how does an explanation work, can you convey such a concept, what points of difficulty arise. Teaching is an experiment. I'm always watching to see how am I getting it across? When the student is interested, it becomes as much a learning experience for the teacher.

Patrick

We were discussing romanticism recently, and asking, What does an adequate response to that actually mean? How much do you need to know about the social and political and geographical change of an entire continent? What's fascinating are the ramifications of experience; hence the necessity to read widely in psychology, sociology, philosophy, history, literature.

Séamas

People think we live in a hermetically sealed cocoon. If only they realized the seething ferment we see around us, and that we try to pick a way across the stepping stones in this morass!

Jimmy Dowds grew up in Donegal and now lives on the Beara peninsula, where he provides much of the energy behind the local exchange trading system (LETS) scheme and runs websites from his caravan. We talked in the LETS shop, surrounded by vegetables, videos, books and clothes. The LETS currency in Beara is called a Hag, after the local goddess.

On the western edge of nowhere

How do people get where they are? Well, in my case, very very bad education. I could hardly write when I left school. I was told I was going to end up in prison. There were about four of us who were the dunces, but those four of us have done quite well. The school system in the sixties didn't know how to deal with what heads we had. Tell us what to do and we'll do the opposite.

So I grew up a rebel. I was always interested in bikes, so that took me away from the mainstream. I had absolutely no interest in football. I could see through a lot of the shit from an early age. One of the things that woke me up way back was books. I liked reading because it was a great escape from the fucking reality I was growing up with. Lyall Watson's *Supernature* really started my head going. I thought, there's another way here.

Where I come from is working class. There were people who went off to college but we never saw them again. When I met professional people later I couldn't believe their lack of suss on what was happening in the world around them, their lack of what I would call intelligence. I thought I was just a stupid fisherman from the west of Ireland. But if you're out on a boat sixty or seventy miles off the coast, you've got to think quick, or you're dead.

So I went fishing, and loved it. Great crack. Money was good one day, back on shore, great party, go out again. Brilliant. Until you end up in a situation where you have to be responsible. Like being a parent. I've two daughters. I tried to stop fishing for a while, living with my ex-wife. It's like a drug, being out on the ocean. You can run off to sea and leave all your problems behind – you can't afford to take them with you. Though I knew I wasn't going to stick with it because I came into fishing in Ireland when it was starting to die. You could see the fish getting scarcer. You knew you were at a funeral.

Where I grew up, my granny had no electricity. People used to come in, play cards and chat – what we call in Donegal, raking. That was nice, I remember sitting in front of the turf fire with me wee cousin, men telling ghost stories and we'd be shaking. There was a closeness between people that disappeared somewhere along the line. I don't have a television, but I know when I walk into people's houses and they're watching it, they're not with you at all.

So how I got to West Cork was, this Spanish boat came into Killybegs looking for an engineer, and I thought it would be nice to go to Spain. Twelve Spaniards and me, we headed off down the west coast. And we got along grand. We came in here with engine trouble, and then, whatever row was going on between the company that owned the boat, and the crew, I didn't understand, but the lads were getting ripped off. So, next thing, they're all sitting on deck, bags packed, telling me they're finished and they're heading home. So I wasn't going to Spain. I was thinking of getting a bus out of here. Went into MacCarthy's bar, and was welcomed, and thought, this is a nice place. There were no buses, of course, till the morning at eight o'clock, so I stayed around, met a few people, stayed for a couple of days, a year. I was up and down between here and Donegal for a while, then came back five or six years ago, this time around with a plan – to live the way I wanted to live.

Community's important, people are important. I like to help people out, do people a favour. I had no notion of economics, had trouble with banks, was in debt, couldn't manage money at all. Some friends of mine were after coming from a conference in Westport about LETS, and they gave me a brochure on it. So I got a few people together, and ended up with everybody looking at me as if I knew what I was talking about when I'd only read one brochure!

jimmy dowds

That was about four years ago. It was like a thing waiting to happen. We're sitting here in the LETS shop, you can see all the stuff there is. What I learned out of LETS is whatever wealth of talent you have among you can stay and grow if you pass it around. Unless you give something away, it doesn't increase. LETS is a way of passing things around with no attachments, no bullshit. Once you put interest on something it has an evil attached to it.

We ask for £5 for running expenses for the office and the rent. But there's no limit to what you can purchase. If you join right now you'll have unlimited credit, you can buy everything that's in here and walk out. You just write a cheque for hags. But they don't exist! It's just a name we chose. So the place is empty, and we've got a huge cheque from you for a couple of thousand hags. Each thing you bought belongs to someone, so that gets spread into their accounts. So all the members become a little bit richer. You're in debt, of course. You can't go down to the bank and take it out. You've got to pay them back by doing whatever it is you do that helps the rest of us. If you bugger off owing two thousand, nothing is going to happen because it's absorbed by the membership. If it happened a lot, it would create inflation. But it doesn't. You get people who move on, but they'd try to bring down their deficit or clear it. If you walk into a bank and ask the bank manager can you trust people, he'll probably say no. Ask anyone in the LETS system and they'll say you can. If you allow people to spend thousands straight away, you place trust in them, and it comes back.

We ask people who want to join LETS, What do you do? They say, Well, I don't know. What are you interested in? I don't know. Have you any hobbies? Is there anything you *like* to do? If you take time with people you'll find they've some wee thing they like doing. So you say to them, offer that, and we'll see will anybody take it up. We produce a directory every few months, listing the skills that people offer – painting houses, fixing cars, whatever. People are very ingenious. There was one woman one year who offered this service where you would tell her all the birthdays of your relatives, all the dates you had to remember, and a few days before she'd remind you that this was coming up. That was a nice wee service to offer.

It's up to the individual to decide what the service is worth. Some people think that a surgeon shouldn't charge any more than someone

on the western edge of nowhere

sewing duvets. I think the individual should decide. When we started the system, people were charging different prices for bread – it could be five, or six, or three hags a loaf, and eventually it balanced out at about three. I wouldn't ask someone what do you think you're worth. You take photographs? That's brilliant. Whatever you want to charge is OK.

On the LETS I fix outboards, lawnmowers, motorbikes, engines. I'll come round and give you a hand with anything. But on the LETS you don't offer as a skill what you do to earn money, you offer something else. You have to be practical, you still need regular currency. What I do for money at the moment involves computers. How long that will last I don't know. But it's a good time, it's a good edge, you meet a lot of people who are living on the edge of society who are into this whole other world that's being created.

We're not completely cut off from other systems. A year or two back I thought if I could get some money from Fás schemes to do what I'm doing anyway, that would be great, and went to see somebody about it. I was ready for a battle, like, What kind of a crazy fucking anarchy are you trying to push here? I walked in and said this is what we're doing and will you back us, and he said, That's brilliant, could you make jobs for a few people? So we were no longer just a few hairy people trading vegetables with each other.

If someone moves down here, it would take six months to get to know people. If you join the LETS, in a couple of months you know most people. You have a list of phone numbers and addresses, and what they do. We've about two hundred people. And there it is for you. In a social sense it's a lifeline.

How do I see the future? At the moment I'm living in a nice place. I own the structure that I'm living in, and hope to buy the piece of land that it's on – with money, not hags. It hasn't got to that yet. But there's a lot of trust around here, people are awake and thinking.

Cormac Boydell is a ceramicist living at the end of a peninsula in the south-west.

Rush and business

The way I grew up was quite isolated. Intellectual Dublin: exhibitions, contemporary art on the walls, a lot of music – but only one kind. We were all sent off to boarding school at the age of seven. There we were were taught that being self-sufficient and independent was a good thing. It's only recently that I've realized that's not how I want to be. So although my habit makes me live in an isolated way, my heart is pulling me out of that. I'm starting to do work with other people now – architects and scientists – which is exciting. Collaborative work gets you into the habit of questioning your own thinking, and listening to other people.

When I first came here I was about twenty-six. I'd studied science, been to Australia, made money, but it didn't make me happy. I came here with romantic ideas about gardens and the simple life, which didn't last long – about six months – then I ran out of money and went to Libya to work on the oil rigs and pay off my debts. I came back to Ireland, learned meditation, which I found amazing, then trained to teach it.

I built my studio in about 1982, and since then I've been in there nine to five and five days a week. I have to impose that rhythm, in order to stop fighting myself about whether or not I've done enough work. I work very hard. I do nearly always what I would choose to do if I were on a pension to do it. I put it out into the world and I sell nearly everything I make. The money I make every year is about as much as I would get on the dole. I don't know what that says. I don't make things with selling in mind. If my heart is in it, it'll sell. I've discovered that.

I love the simplicity of ceramics. The Zen idea of just gathering water and chopping wood. I like those great Japanese craftspeople who just did one very simple thing, very beautiful, with none of this razzmatazz of being an international artist.

I was fifty last March, and I went to Ladakh. Now there's a community that's not driven. One of the Tibetan Buddhist Four Thoughts is the equality of all living beings. At Ladakh I was treated like a fellow human being, no more, no less. I found it very inspiring. Success is measured so materially nowadays. When people ask me how I'm doing I always say things like: I've got lots of commissions, lots of people are buying my work. I'd rather say that I go into my studio every day really excited to carry on with what I was doing the previous day. We're so consumed by rush and business. I think we have to go backwards.

We can't just go on measuring our success by our consumption. The wealth of the northern hemisphere is dependent on the poverty of the southern. We have to at least aspire to equality of human beings. The habit of our society is not to think about what money is, just to consume. 'Spiritual' has become a disturbing word. I think it's very helpful that there's a spiritual nadir now; organized religion needs to go bankrupt, it's in cahoots with the material world.

I came here because it seemed like home. People who come down here say, What a beautiful place, and I say, Oh, I've forgotten. Anyway, I'm not here solely for the beauty, though it remains a great healer.

When I first came here, there was no electricity or running water, but there was a community. A lot of the houses were lived in by people who'd lived in them for generations. On Sunday we'd walk out, and into one another's houses. We'd sit mostly in silence, or have a cup of tea, chat, watch the fire.

We visted the Goggins several times over the summer,
four generations in seven caravans on a road outside
Blarney. We talked to old Ma and old Da, Rosey and
Jimmy Goggin. We went back in September, after
they'd gone, and found the County Council JCB pil-
ing earth along the edge of the road to make sure the
travellers wouldn't be back next year.

Anything strange or comical?

Sometimes of course when it's raining you think, what kind of life is this?
says Rosey. But you've got the freedom, you're outdoors all the time. There's
the river just down there, and the boys made up the bank so there's a swimming place, one here for the women and children, and another down the
river for the boys. Generations of us have been doing this: settled in the
winter – Wexford, we're all from Wexford – and on the road in the summer. We all get together in the summer. This is a really good spot here.
We've been here a few years now; used to be nearer in to the city but it's
better out here, the guards don't bother you. If they know you've an address
they leave you alone. Did you ever know any travellers where you grew up?

It's not like in olden times, *says Jimmy from the front seat of the Hiace, where*
he's listening to the news. In olden times you didn't have to keep the door
locked. These days if you slip out and leave the door open, when you come
back there's nothing to shut the door on! In olden times you had the freedom. You didn't need to be a scholar. Where are all the scholars now?
They're in the prison on Spike Island, they're down at the Social Security.
He takes hold of the steering wheel. Everything I know is in here. *Taps his*
temple. Them two teachers I had at school, two women, they had us outside collecting wood while all the girls in the class learned to read and
write. I can't read or write.

He was always mitching, *says Rosey.* Would you like to buy some perfume? I've some very good perfume.

We've eight sons and two daughters. Reared on a mountain up in Kilkenny. And we've loads of grandchildren. And one great-grandson, little Gerry. He's the one out there lying on the road. I'm also looking after six children whose mother died, God rest her. We all get on, never argue, the boys get on grand. They're out with the vans, and the women are back in the trailers, cleaning the windows, looking after the childer, cooking, you know, the usual. Weekends we go down to the Waterloo Inn and have a bit of a singsong. And of course we all go up to Ballinasloe in October. It's a great crack. Was you ever up in Ballinasloe?

The children can't get enough of the camera. They're striking poses and their mothers are wiping noses and whipping a frock onto the baby and setting her on the rocking horse. And there's the piebald mare with her feathers fluffed out. Big Sarge wants a picture of himself holding the foal. And Billy-go-backwards goes backwards, out of the picture.

Conal Creedon is trying to sell a laundrette he's run for five years. He has a play in his head that's waiting to get out, as well as a radio series and a book of stories that have already escaped.

Will the parachute open?

At a certain point in their lives people start to have an insight into what it's all about. For me it's not about an awful lot. The earth is like a lifeboat, there's nowhere to jump when this thing gets banjaxed up. We're just flying around in this big abyss and people don't realize that this *is* the lifeboat; there's meanies drilling holes in the corner, and the rest of us are too caught up in painting the boat to notice.

I'm chasing my own tail as far as generating a lifestyle is concerned. Like starting the laundrette. I'd been in Canada for a few years doing a degree in economics. I got married, got into daddy mode you could say, came back to Ireland, bought this building from my family; I had all the machines in and I really didn't want to open. Then one day Denis the Chinaman brought his washing in and just went in and did it himself; and then I had to open. The laundrette was a job, and I didn't really want a job – I still don't. That's why I'm selling it. It's not really in order to go writing – though there's three plays I've got in my head. You're interviewing somebody who's giving up. I surrender! Don't shoot, I'm coming in, lads!

I'm very self-sufficient, and spend a lot of time knocking around on my own – when I get the chance. People call round a lot here. I don't want possessions. You can have a garden in order to enjoy it, but if you have a garden in order to be seen to have a garden, you're paying for the lifestyle rather than living the life. You can spend a lot of time getting the right sequence of ducks on the wall, making your stage set around you. I think St Francis had it all together really – not that I'm a churchy head at all – he got rid of a lot of things, lost a lot of friends, and said, This is the way I'm going, all right? I'm not talking hairshirt, though, I'd want some possessions – a good radio, maybe a CD player. I'm chasing very little, really. I'm not breaking down any barriers and getting out. I grew up having the freedom to say, right, I'm popping my clogs, this is the road I'm going. Independence isn't a revelation, it's just a way of life.

I do feel I'm always watching, even now, I'm listening to everything you're not saying. When you click into the fact that you're capable of watching what's around you, it's like an addiction. I am part of things as well, though; I grew up here, I know everybody. I'm really not worried about what happens when I sell the laundrette. I'm just going to jump out of the aeroplane and hope the parachute opens. I really feel – and this probably goes back to pre-Famine times – that once the roof is over my head I'll be fine.

Judith Evans and Arthur Watson were among the founders of the East Clare Community Co-op and the Steiner school in Scarriff. They make posters and put on puppet shows.

Ding ding, we're off again

Judith

When we were at university in Coleraine, we didn't feel any urgency or responsibility. I felt that my education was teaching me to learn, and that in that sense it was a success.

Arthur

I wanted to get as much out of my education as possible. It was like an appetite, an end in itself. We started two magazines – called *P* and *PS*. And in the theatre area too, there were always little things happening. That was what the university situation provided. There wasn't any thought of career structure. My parents were working-class Belfast, so they had the struggle from the working class to the middle class, and any education I got would push me nearer to being a teacher or a lawyer. I quickly sussed out this was not for me.

Judith

When we finished at university we went to London, and then went to live on a commune in Norfolk. I went in thinking, Now I will have such close relationships with all these people, but in fact it's a microcosm of the real world – you get on really well with some, and can't bear others, and learn to tolerate them.

Arthur

All the way through late teenage years I had a wish to join or identify with a group, and because I couldn't find it in normal life, I looked to the commune. It was like doing your PhD in social anthropology!

Judith

After the commune we moved back to London and worked with my father, who painted murals. I suspect he looked at us and thought, They haven't got any direction, and said, Look, would you like to come and give me a hand. We worked with him for three years, and it was like a kind of apprenticeship. So that was our informal training in art, which we started to use when we came here twenty years ago.

Arthur

London seemed to be becoming an amazing place, though it was also beginning to feel very environmentally damaged. This was in the mid-seventies. We had our first daughter, Bella, by then. So the question was: do we get a mortgage, *be* someone, or do we get out? Also my father got ill, so we went to Belfast to be with him. There was a cluster of things really, the birth of Bella, my father's illness and death – and work changed. Jobs weren't coming in. It seemed an opportunity to do what all our friends were saying: Must get to Ireland sometime – but we've never seen them here!

Judith

Some friends of ours who did decide to get out came to this cottage, which was derelict then. They stayed here for a couple of years, and we came over to join them, but then they went off to Colombia and we moved in here.

Arthur

It just happened to be here. It could have been Cork or Donegal. Somewhere in the west. It was very remote, it still is. At first there weren't many people at all, just you and me it seemed, and you cried and I got paralyzed! We just thought, what are we doing? In any change you make there is a strong element of apprehension, of fear. But the need to go on, the need to find out, is stronger.

Judith

If you start off with very little money you don't carry the same kind of risks as people who think about doing these things when they've got a bit of money. They're afraid they might lose it. We came over with a car and what it would hold. And for years that was all we had.

Arthur

We never wanted to acquire much. In my childhood we didn't have much, and what we had went around, and those ideas have carried through. It's better to share. For younger people today I think there's a huge aspiration and struggle to acquire things. Most of my friends weren't like that. And most of the people I've identified with haven't been like that.

When I was in Coleraine, Jimmy Simmons was a big influence. He was the only lecturer who was open. You could go back to his place at two in the morning and talk about Bob Dylan. He let us mark our own papers. He was an old-fashioned revolutionary. Another great influence – on setting up the co-op especially – was a man called Pat Fleming, who was moving round Ireland like a whirlwind. He was very into co-ops and he pushed us very firmly in that direction.

The co-op started in this room. We had meetings all through the winter of 1987–88, five of us. None of us liked the idea of a structure that went from the top down. The co-op operates community employment schemes – not just digging holes in the road or tidying graveyards, but painters, seed-savers, coppicers, weavers, basket-makers. Whatever energies people bring in, we help them. The puppets started through the co-op and was supported by it. The co-op provides a way of dealing with the normal world. It helps marginalized people who can't easily establish an identity, who don't have a proper name, who wouldn't be able to get funding for their projects.

Judith

Another push behind the starting of the co-op was the Steiner school. It had already started, and we needed some way of fund-raising. Later it was decided that it wasn't a good idea for the two things to be in the one organization, and that it would be much better for the co-op to help parents raise their own income, rather than the parents contributing free labour. Of course you have to get involved with structures that exist, Fás schemes and

ding ding, we're off again

so on, but the people in the co-op have found over the years that they can change the way things work, simply by challenging it. Which is very satisfying.

Arthur

The local community are gradually beginning to understand the use of the co-op. We've always had an environmental profile. We did a clean-up campaign on the lakes, illegal dumping, waste from animals and so on. We discovered that Finsa – the chipboard factory in Scarriff – were producing fourteen times the EU allowable level of particles in the smokestack and dropping them on the town. Through pressure and scientific help, we succeeded in getting it to seven times the allowable level, and to install a chimney. Sometimes still, when the wind is bad, you walk through Scarriff and it's like Victorian London, there's a mist, and a stink from the formaldehyde particles.

Judith

Over the time we've been here, there has been a much more green outlook. In a way it is a drop in the ocean, but hopefully the education the children get in the school will contribute to a change. The ethos of the school in Scarriff is very much head, heart, hands. There's no headmaster or headmistress. Teachers are thought of as creative people, and the children's creativity and imagination are more emphasized than their intellect. They learn to write before they learn to read. The first reading they do is what they've written.

Arthur

Growing up in Belfast, what I regarded as normal was Protestant supremacy disguised as democracy – in a nutshell. I began to realize, this is a crazy society. It's not normal, it's completely abnormal. I'd no legitimacy once I discovered the king had no clothes. I kept saying, This guy is naked, this is terrible, this is wonderful, why aren't we all naked? I see so much distortion in normal society that normality for me is what I am and what I do.

In the west of Ireland there is a madness, an eccentricity, I think, where reality and unreality, time and timelessness mix and merge freely. If you keep fixing things all the time, like having a job and a rhythm, maybe the ribbon of your life can be kept quite straight. Or maybe it's quite dishevelled, more of a river than a ribbon, like, to be in the swim, or in a canal – no, it has to be a river, and suddenly you go round a bend, it's a waterfall and you go, oh God! I thought I was a puppeteer. Oh no, I'm not a puppeteer any more.

Judith
I sometimes have a yearning to be something specific.

Arthur
You are something specific to me!

Judith
For some people a job can be a lifeline because it gets you away from thinking about all that.

Arthur
When people get a job they automatically get a purpose. I remember when we were on the commune I spent a week feeling worried. Like, what are we doing here lads? Everybody in the outside world seems to be busy, buzzing up and down the A10 to London. I remember lying in bed, looking out the door and realizing I'd fallen into purposelessness.

As soon as you enter purposelessness, society tells you you're in jeopardy, you're in shadowland. It's a difficult thing to send anybody off into that, without them knowing that that's what they're doing. It would help them to know that they're doing it and that it's OK. A lot of people get damaged, and rush back into purposefulness.

Not to have a purpose is to have control. Our society is so full of function and purpose that you're not really safe to ask questions. We often thought in the school that it would be a good idea to have a moratorium, a day when all teaching stopped. A freeing up from all politicking, all machinations, and just come to grips with questions like, What is the purpose of education? A reflection day. And then, ding ding, we're off again.

ding ding, we're off again

John O'Neill and his wife Catriona bought the old railway station in Lismore, County Waterford, two years ago. They moved from Belfast, where John had a hi-fi business. They're restoring the station buildings and, in the old goods shed, John runs courses on woodwork, basket-making, stone-walling and ironwork, using traditional methods and home-made tools.

Going backwards

I don't ever remember learning woodwork. I went to a very middle-class school where they definitely didn't want people doing things like that. So I was curious about it, I tinkered with it, and then I got into the idea of woodturning using old methods. I thought, I'll build a lathe myself, rather than buying a shiny electric one, which will soon wear out anyway. I became very interested in the archaeology and history of woodwork. It's not the machinery itself that fascinates me, more the traditional methods which relied on the skill of the operator – whereas modern machinery tends to replace those skills, often with an inferior result. A lot of skills are being lost. An example would be the mouldings on the shelves people were making at the carpentry class you were at last week. Most of those mouldings would now be produced by machine. You can now buy about a dozen mouldings. But years ago when carpenters made their own mouldings there would have been thousands of them. They used their imagination and just made them up. There was a huge variety of mouldings, some of them very beautiful.

Nowadays there's uniformity everywhere, in everything you touch. It's one of the reasons behind the nostalgia people have for country furniture, for anything old. These things represent the days when people had more skills and were wiser. There is this notion that people in the past knew more, that they understood their life better, that life was simpler, and they didn't screw things up in quite the way that modern people do. It's partly a fallacy that people were happier or better off, but you can take the best of the past, and the learning of skills is part of that. But there's lots of things I like about the modern world.

There was one person on the last woodwork course who was a programmer from Microsoft, who'd never done any woodwork before. She heard about us on the Internet, which is a funny contradiction. She made her bookshelf, took it home with her, and wrote us a thank-you letter saying how pleased she was with it. What she does every day is very much more complicated than making shelves, but not necessarily very satisfying, so to get away from it and work with your hands is a real break.

Some people who come on courses here do so with a view to setting up a business. Fifty per cent of the people who want to learn stone-walling, for example, want to earn a living doing that. Mostly people are not thinking of earning a living through learning new skills. I would like it if they were. And some people are happy just to learn. There was one man on the last woodwork course who came on his bike, and couldn't take home the shelf he'd made. He said that didn't matter, because it wasn't the product that was important, but the experience of making it, and that pleased me.

A lot of people feel very strongly about the thing they take home, and I can understand that. We design that into as many courses as possible, because people want to have the symbol. You do get people who do courses all the time, in practically anything, four or five a year, with no intention of following them up. They like gatherings, the social set, and you do meet a lot of really nice people in the craft area, very relaxed people. I must say that in the past six or seven years of being involved in the craft area, I've met more people who've become friends than I did in fifteen years of working in the hi-fi business.

We're not funded by anyone. We looked at the Leader funding, but they didn't know when they'd be getting their money, and I just couldn't wait for them to make up their minds. It made much more sense for us to get into business a year early than to wait for them. I'm a bit critical of the schemes anyway. Even people who organize those schemes admit that it's just a way of injecting money into the economy.

I don't see myself as an idealist. I'm a businessman in the sense that I hope to make some money somewhere down the line. I have theories about business, for example that businesses which integrate themselves into the community survive much better. So as much for business as for any other reason, we're setting up this centre with a very wide mandate. We want to involve craftspeople in the area. We want to have exhibitions, and provide work-spaces so that people can make things here, and sell them themselves. I don't want to run a shop. What I'd like to see in five or six years is a whole co-op of people making baskets, selling them here and elsewhere. If I achieve that, I won't actually make direct money out of that, but at the same time people will come to this place and interest will grow.

There is a possibility for people to make a living from traditional skills. What you need is a catalyst, someone who's encouraging people in that direction. It's easier to be a catalyst when you move in from somewhere else. It would be a hard thing to do in a place where everybody knows you. Most people won't take risks unless there's someone encouraging them, and even then it's hard if you have a family. Though having parents who are fighting all the time because they hate what they're doing is probably worse than having parents who don't have much money.

I like physical work and I like working with my hands. I like working under pressure. There is a stigma attached to working with your hands. It's easier for me, though, because I did go to university. I studied mechanical engineering – even if I did leave in my final year, out of boredom. I've been in businesss. It's easier to turn round and do something socially less acceptable when you've got that under your belt. It's not that I set out deliberately not to conform. But I often say that I don't quite catch what I'm supposed to be doing. I don't quite understand what society expects of me.

A lot of people are blowing into areas of Ireland bringing lots of ideas. Local people see the ones that succeed and they get involved. For example, nearly all the first cheese-makers were foreigners, and now there's a sizeable cheese industry, and half or more than half of them are Irish. And that's happening in lots of different fields. So going backwards isn't always a bad thing.

going backwards

Judith and Jeremiah Hoad live on a hill in Donegal, a mile from the nearest neighbour. For thirty years they have chosen to live without electricity, plumbing, or a kitchen sink. 'It's a bucket economy,' Jeremiah says. 'Everything goes in or out of the door in a bucket, and we carry it.' Jeremiah is a painter, and Judith currently practises Shen Tao healing, writes books and runs workshops.

Welcome to the bucket economy

Medicine is the latest in a long list of things I do. It may be the final one. I was a dressmaker when I first met Jerry – I was Judith of Canterbury. I went backwards from there: I learned to weave, I learned to spin, I learned to shear. I also wrote about these things and taught them. I got interested in herbs about thirty years ago, then thought wasn't I an awful eejit not to be using it, so I started using it on the kids, and it worked, it was brilliant. Then I learned about homeopathy, and rescue remedy, and the Bach flower remedies, and people used to come and say, would you ever make me a bottle of this, or do you know anything about so and so. If I was asked, I always did, and I never charged anything for it because it wasn't my livelihood.

I think most people find what they want by discovering what they don't want. That's certainly the way I did it. My school life was happier than my home life. I had quite a good head for academic subjects, together with a great desire to use my hands. My mother wasn't particularly adept – of course she knitted. Dad wanted me to be articled to a solicitor. I wanted to do things and make things.

One thing I discovered at school was that I had no competitive sense. I remember two events on the sports field when I must have been eleven years old. We had an elderly games teacher called Zoe Roe who was lecturing us about something on the netball field. This wonderful school was built in 1938, and went down steep fields and then there was the railway, and then the Medway. In those days there were barges on the Medway, and I was glued to the fence watching the barges, half-profile to this woman, and she caught me at it and sent me to watch the barges for the rest of the term. She didn't know what she'd done because it was far more fun than playing bloody netball. My mother insisted that I knit my own knee-socks, so I used to wear my blazer, which was forbidden, in the goal net of the hockey field, and knit my sock until the ball came anywhere near me.

I'm naturally a rebel. If somebody sets something up, I find a way of talking it the other way. I like a good argument! Eventually I suppose that began to percolate through to my deeper sense, and I decided I was going to do it my way. Then it came to a fulcrum point where I was doing it because I was going to do it and I didn't care who didn't like it. Then Jerry and I teamed up and we were doing it together. Which was quite novel for both of us. Then I suddenly turned round one day and discovered that what I'd been doing all these years was something that other people were interested to find that someone was doing. It's turned around from being something you didn't talk about very much unless you wanted to get into a fight, to something that's desirable, particularly amongst the young. They come and see how we've managed it all these years, living for thirty years without modern amenities.

In 1967 Jerry stopped teaching. After that, everything was easy. He was giving up all that inculcation about 'you have to work so you'll get a pension'. We even thought in those days that by the time we were eligible for old-age pensions there might not be one. Society was crumbling around our ears, so why subscribe to it?

You have to work harder if you don't have a machine to do it. Life is slower, which isn't a bad thing at all. Instead of the instant light switch, we have to pump up a paraffin lamp and light candles. Make sure we've got paraffin. Keep the lamps clean.

We felt that if you have to work at the business of living, like carrying water, carrying fuel, removing slops and removing ashes and so on, it keeps the body fit and it keeps the mind in the right focus. Education teaches kids that there's no dignity in the labour that wears a blue coat, but there is in a white coat, and better still to wear your own suit and be at the top. I don't buy into that at all. My notion is that it's the people who demean the work, not the work that demeans the people. Education educates kids not to stay at home. They get qualified to do things that they can only do somewhere else, serving the system somewhere else. They're not taught to build a house, do carpentry, dig a potato patch, go fishing.

In the wintertime we do more chores than in the summertime. In the winter even when it's dark we get up about eight, and we work till about ten or eleven. We wash up once a day, in the morning. We bring the water in, and the fuel. We've got the range cleaned out and fire laid or lit. There's the studio fire to do. There's the post to collect. There's the drinking water to collect – quarter of a mile down the hill. All those things are done at the beginning of the day. And when that's over, we can go for whatever we want to do. Jerry might be painting, I might be writing, or collecting herbs, or making boxes.

We've never proselytized. Years ago there was no point. When people come here, they have to see that this is our way of doing things. They have to find what they want to do in the way that it suits them. But they recognize that you can opt out of the system – even if you can't do it a hundred per cent. For example, we take our washing to a friend with a washing machine, and she does our laundry on the LETS system every week. I think what they find when they get here is that it's all right to be an individual. It's all right not to have those things that say, Look, I can afford this kind of car, this kind of house. They find what they can do without. We always tell people what to expect before they come. For example they've got to dig a hole in the garden if they want to have a crap. There's a basic requirement that when they've done that they wash their hands with soap and water. When you live simply you've got to observe some simple rules.

We've lived in two houses without electricity or plumbing, one in Wales and one here. Originally we didn't have electricity because it wasn't there. Then we got used to living without it, and no longer had the appliances that require it. It would cost a fortune if we had this place wired. We'd have to buy a hoover, a washing machine, a toaster, all the things that would justify having it. When we came here we made it even simpler than we had in Wales, where we had pretentions towards having a drain. We had a water barrel in the kitchen there. But here we don't have any of that. We don't have a kitchen sink. People live here now, around us, our neighbours,

welcome to the bucket economy

who'd always lived like that, a few of them still do. But they lived like that at the beginning of their lives. It doesn't faze them at all. Sometimes it alarms local people, women in particular, to see that people they consider educated, foreign and exotic were actually going for the trap of a hard, simple life. But it isn't a trap when you choose it voluntarily.

Our daily life is not just a question of choice, it's a question of mindfulness. If you take the hoover you can whizz it around the floor. But if you take a brush, you're down on your knees – that's why you're in here without shoes, because that's how I clean the floor – you're mindful of the person who wove the rug. We carry our drinking water a quarter of a mile from downhill, so we're mindful of it, we don't wash in it. We've got plenty of washing water that comes off the roof. We strip-wash every day in half a gallon of water in a bowl.

My contention about cleanliness is that it isn't the facilities you have, it's your outlook. You do the best with what you've got. We deliberately brought up our kids that way, because we felt that reading aloud together at night, playing games in front of the fire, when other people were sitting in front of a screen, we were having much more fun, and generating the imagination. It was hard for our children because we chose to live the way we do, they didn't choose, and they missed things their contemporaries had, like television. But I think long-term it will be an advantage. At the moment they live with electricity, television, all mod cons. It's their choice. One daughter said to me, This is real, this is how we are, this is today. Though it has to be said that when our grandchildren come here, they love it, because it's different. They can draw on the concrete floor with chalk.

I think there's a special link between children and their grandparents. It's so sad that that structure has been lost. With the extended family, it would be the young parents who were out in the fields and away in the forest or whatever, and the little ones would be at home with the grandparents who would do the quiet domestic things, passing on all those wisdoms they'd learned. These days you have the much-reviled nuclear family which is the last remnant of the extended family. Until Yale locks came, nobody's doors were locked around here. We didn't have a key here for at least ten years. There was a sense of freedom and accessibility. Now, our society has become so corrupt, personal identity has disappeared for so many people that they're breaking out, and unable to control their emotions. If you love someone and care for them, you're unable to go up to a stranger and swing a hammer at them, it's not in you to do it.

We've chosen isolation in our two homes of the last thirty years. We're still in the full of our health, we can still do all that needs to be done, but we have isolated ourselves from community. We now have a notion in our heads of a house we want to build. We call it the Snail House, a round house with a spiral structure inside. We want it to be among people of like mind – and they probably won't be blood relatives – because we feel that we are going to need physical support. We would like somebody living within hailing distance who is of another generation, whose kids can come, because we have experience, we have skills, we have a library.

When we were young and energetic and could do all those things for ourselves, that was fine, but we have slowed down a bit, and we have to think about these things. Jerry's seventy-three, and has a heart condition. I'm nearly sixty. I look around at people my age, and I see the skin like orange peel, and it's so sad, because what happens in the body has also happened in the mind.

Life is a terminal condition; people don't realize that because it's been blotted out in our culture. We have life wills printed out and pinned to the door about all we don't want to have happen. Like going into hospital. Die happy, die at home! I do think society could be different because society has been different. People like to think that progress is continual and even, that we're better today than we were yesterday. It's absolute rubbish.

When I was ten or eleven years old I kept mice. I had a black mouse, a white mouse and a parti-coloured mouse, and I bred mice, I used to sell them to the cleaners at school – shilling a time. I found that if I allowed my mice all inhabit the same space, I didn't get young. If I separated them out in pairs, I did. I didn't understand at that age, I just saw what happened, if you put them all in together they didn't breed. Most of the learning I've done has been like that. The learning has come before the realization.

Real reality

I always had a great old driving force to find out more about life. I was always into the natural world, I wanted to understand how things worked. At school they were always trying to discourage me – they said it was a waste of time. I've come to think we're a very destructive lot on this planet, and we can't afford to stay ignorant. We feel powerful because we know how to alter things on a whim or a fancy. We're very good at justifying what we do, but we don't have strong codes. We're very numerous on this planet and we're crowding and spoiling life systems we haven't properly understood yet. But we're still in an optimistic period, we could now restore things, create environments in which life forms can renew themselves.

I don't think of myself as an independent – I just do what I do. I try as gently as possible to emphasize through the media the interdependence of things – and the need for an education system that allows education to happen. Most education is a closed circuit. Sideways thinking and new ideas are not encouraged. You won't get your high marks if you come up with something fresh and healthy. Most teachers are too sacred about their ideas; they can't bear to admit they're wrong, that they might have to alter their thinking. My parents would always say that once you start saying something is definitely the case, you're wrong. You have to stray off the beaten track every day of the week in order to stay on the track at all.

I'm not a loner, I'm quite gregarious, I like parties, I like to have people around, animals, all sorts of life forms. This place is like a microclimate, you know, the glen is so deep the rain always falls straight down, and the sun collects down here and heats the place like a tropical rainforest. The old ironworks used to employ fifteen people, and now I rent out studios to artists, I keep a few animals. People bring me things all the time, I'm always minding critters of some sort. It might be a snake, a tarantula, a puppy or a pigeon with broken wings. They know I'll know what to do. And I do a bit of broadcasting and consultancy work; I go round schools giving talks. I have one young fella myself. Of course I would have liked to have ten kids. I like babies round the place, baby animals, baby humans. Maybe I'm a frustrated daddy. I like life, and all the intricacies that go with it.

('I used to hate nature at school,' says Sinéad – she lives across the road and comes up the glen most days with her friend Catharina – 'but now it's my favourite lesson.')

The people who live with real reality are hard to find, people who are in balance with their lot, and have a good philosophy – and they're hard to produce. There are lots of children in this neighbourhood, and lots of trees; the children have never climbed the trees to see what they can see from the top. When we were kids we climbed all the trees and explored everything thoroughly. Every kind of exploring was part of our lifestyle. In our family we tend to give each other credit for who we are, we've never been critical of others who might be different. Prejudice and fear go hand in hand – fear and lack of understanding too. If you explore, you don't end up afraid of things. Of course you'd have a healthy respect for things that were going to recycle you, but you wouldn't be afraid of something just because it was unusual. I'm very interested in anything that frightens me – I didn't like heights so I took up sky-diving. I've gone all sorts of ways towards learning things. I can cut out a jacket and sew it up. I was skipper of a research ship on the Great Barrier Reef. I have a licence to drive a mule underground! That was from a copper, lead and zinc mine in Australia, four thousand feet underground. I've got licences for land, sea and air. I can throw people out of aeroplanes officially. I'm never stuck! If I found myself on the street tomorrow, I'd know what to do, I'd soon be back into things.

I've lived in all the houses in the glen – I'm always in the house that needs the most doing to it. I used to have a back bathroom in this place, but then a couple of parrots fell in love so I gave it to them. I'm doing up the house at the back of the glen, and it's nearly ready. Next time you come you can stay in the North Wing! There'll be five bedrooms, and a library – there's a zoology book I'd like to write – and all the old ironwork from the mill I'll leave as part of the lounge – can't you imagine a sofa built up around that old cam? I don't mind all the work. You need something to let your mad blood loose.

We respect each other's privacy here. I wouldn't call in on my neighbour who's right next door, I'd phone first. We have a policy that people stay on the main track running through the glen. The other side of the river, people and dogs and cats are kept out; otters and foxes and all kinds of things are stretched out in the sun over there in full view for us to observe; they know we never go over there and that's their piece of ground and we don't encroach on them. Maybe they're wondering why! Children playing in a canoe go as far as a stone in the river and not further. They know there's otters and that we don't go into their area. That's so important. They can have full enjoyment of the river – they're squealing away, they're splashing around, they're sinking the boat – but they do it in their patch. It's no good just telling them not to go down there. Why? Just because I say so. That doesn't work. I suggest to them there's another form of life down there that requires no disturbance. And then the kids are able to see the otters, and hear them whistle to each other in the night and that's a lovely richness to live in.

real reality

Coolmountain is a West Cork community of a hundred people, with another fifty transient on the fringes. There are two shops, a community centre, and a scattering of houses people have built themselves, as well as tepees, benders, caravans and old buses.

Voices from Coolmountain

Katrin and Mike and their three children live in the Dome, the original house of the community, a geodesic dome built in the early seventies. They have lived in Coolmountain for ten years. Mike is a thatcher and Katrin makes baskets. We talked to Katrin.

My dream is not to owe anything, to be in charge of where I am and have all the freedom I want. I know that everything can crumble under my feet and this place will still be here. My parents didn't understand why I didn't want to marry someone like a teacher and have a really secure life. They still think I'm mad! They can't relate to me getting up in the morning and saying, Oh, what shall I do today? Maybe I'll make a basket, maybe I'll make two, maybe I won't make any. That sort of vagueness freaks them out. It's got to be eight o'clock breakfast and then the whole day totally mapped out. My priorities are different. For example, my children can walk out of here, and two hours later they're not back, and I'm not worried about them. I know that all the neighbours will look after them. That's an amazing freedom.

People who go to the bank and take out a loan to buy the things they want, haven't actually achieved them. We've achieved everything we have here. We all want to improve our lifestyle, but we're prepared to do it slowly and we want to keep it simple. We really wanted to have running water in the house – I didn't mind taking nappies down to the stream for a winter or two, but there came a point when enough was enough, I want water in the house. So we did it ourselves, fitted all the bits together, and when the water came out we shouted, Look at this! We've done it! We found a bath in a ditch, painted it up, and it was lovely. The satisfaction is wonderful. No plumber would look at it and say it was done properly. If a tadpole gets stuck in a pipe I can actually go up there and fix it myself. I've got my own well. It's a privilege beyond almost anything to have your own clean water.

I'm not going to be here for ever, oh no. I'm looking forward to the next stage. There will come a point in my life when I'll want to travel, get a motorbike and go to India. I've done the sex, drugs and rock 'n' roll bit, now I'm doing the family bit, and then the third part to look forward to is travel – that'll be my exploring time, learning time. Not that I'm sitting around now being bored. I enjoy my kids. I've created my own employment. I've found something I love doing – making baskets. I do love it, that's a great gift. I love knowing I can make anything I want. Kids are told so often they can't do things. I'll always try things. I don't care if I'm not very good.

I'm not particularly interested in persuading people to live as I do. Everybody has to find their own path. I can say to people: you could try this, and maybe there is more to life than getting into debt buying a new car. I'm not saying that what I'm doing is right, just that it's right for me, it's what I want to do, how I want to live.

In the beginning, when someone wanted to come and live here, we would sit in here in a circle, and people would say what they wanted to do. It had to be all right with everybody – there wasn't one case where we said no. But as people started to own their bit of land, and let other people come and stay on it, it became impossible to control – which is great in its own way.

It's funny to look back and feel sentimental about the days when there were so few of us here. The community side of things doesn't matter so much to me any more, though there's still a core of people I totally trust. We didn't come here to start a community, we just came here and the community happened. I think there's probably a pattern in communities: coming together, the excitement of creating a new garden, creating a new life, creating new children – the time we had on our hands, we just partied, it was bliss! We couldn't believe our luck. That we could be out here. And nobody bothered us. It was fantastic! It's like a couple coming together, it's full of love, it's wonderful. And then comes the point where there's a plateau, like now. And then what next?

There did come a point when there was a huge influx of people – travellers – and certainly there was a distance between them and the people who have settled on the mountain. We didn't get a grip on it, we should have made a much bigger effort, so as not to lose what we'd created. Not that that's why I think I'll go off travelling one day. I don't want to leave here with any negative feelings. I'd rather stay and work them out. I'd want to be able to come back and have people say, Great! there's Katrin!

Moira and John and their daughter Emmy live in a wooden kit house put up by a group of them in four days. Their son Jake lives up the hill in a bus. We talked to Moira.

We were young in the sixties and early seventies, and that was a time when people did start to think, hang on, maybe I don't want to be a chartered accountant. In those days you could just get on the Magic Bus to go to India after doing a factory job to get the money. We drove a twenty-year-old Volkswagen all the way to Delhi. Four of us. In those days you could do things like that. It was great to go away for the winter and see how other people lived. When I was young my father was in the Air Force, so I moved every two years. I'm afraid it just gets addictive.

But it's great to be here now and know I don't have to go anywhere if I don't want to. We've never owned our own house before. We bought this field, but we're the guardians of it as far as I'm concerned, and we can protect it as much as we can, by being careful about not putting chemicals on the land, making sure nothing horrible happens here.

I think community is a better way to live, sharing, and giving support. We're lucky we've got such a mixed bunch of people, and that we don't have any common guru or aim. You have to be allowed to be individual, but you can't do something that upsets everybody else. Everybody's got to feel happy about being here. I think we have to take responsibility

voices from coolmountain

for our own community. Nobody wants to be a policeman, but you can't allow people to hurt themselves or each other.

The community grew in a very haphazard way. After Katrin bought the fourteen acres of Dome land, the two local farmers weren't averse to selling little fields that bordered the fourteen acres. And Katrin invited a few people to live on her land, and then they bought their own bit. Because the farmers were willing to sell a field for a thousand pounds, or a few hundred pounds in the early days, that was the reason people came here.

Most people felt they could be more themselves, or how they'd like to be, here. We lived in a truck in England. That got to be tricky in Thatcher's Britain! So we decided to come here. My sister lived here in the early seventies. I'd been to visit and really liked the peace and quiet, and the greenness and the fresh air and the clean water, all those things that strike you when you first come. And a kind of easiness. Nobody was rushing about the place. You could be slow if you wanted to. And one thing that really amazed me when we came was that people didn't judge you for living in a truck, or being a bit colourful in your clothes. It was what you were like and how you behaved.

Irish people have a strong community spirit, they care for old people, especially in the country. I think a lot of the local people understand how we live, and how we think, especially the old people. Their lives have changed so drastically in the last fifteen years or so. There were hardly any cars when we first came here, and the ones that were there were all tied up with baler twine. Now everybody's got a posh car, and there's rules and regulations about everything. But they don't like people telling them what to do and what to think, and they understand that that's why we're here.

Between St Francis' Hall and a sweet shop is Neff's plaster works, figurines and cornicing. A workshop, full of chipped effigies, is dimly lit except for Jim's bench.

The madonna man

Neff. The name is German, the grandfather came over in the 1860s, a watchmaker – they were looking for watchmakers in Ireland then – and the father was a watchmaker too.

Jim, now eighty-two, has been painting plaster madonnas since 1925 when he left the Crawford School of Art. It was different then, more bohemian, *he says, mixing flesh tones on his madonna's cheek.* I still paint for my own pleasure, too, landscapes, in pastel.

Jim Neff is a small man. He works standing at a bench, the floor slowly building up over the years with bits of plaster, so that as he has grown older and smaller, the ground has risen up to meet him.

Business goes up and down too. It depends on the climate of the times. There was a big slump after Vatican II; and then again with all the moving statues at the end of 1986. I've been trying to retire for three or four years, but the work keeps coming in. It's nice to be wanted, but now I really am retiring. Well, I'm really trying to. I wouldn't want to hazard a guess how many statues I've painted. Thousands. What am I going to do when I've painted the last madonna? Let out a cheer, I should think. Do some more painting, probably. It's very peaceful, painting.

He moves slowly, talks softly. The madonna's cheek is a demure pink all over; he works in a darker tone under her ear. There are statues everywhere, ready, unready, abandoned, crumbled; heads, arms, peeling limbs on shelves among pots of paint. One large crate is waiting to travel out to a Catholic Mission in Papua New Guinea. On the counter by the door are several small statues with plastic bags over their heads.

Is there anyone to take over from me? No, I've one son who's gone in for chemistry, and another who works in the forestry. But there is another fella doing the plasterwork over by the Mercy Hospital.

Is he religious himself?
Nothing abnormal, *he says.*

No, I don't mind being photographed. Maybe the madonnas give you a stillness. Lots of people have come in over the years, there must be photographs of me all over the world. The last photo has me standing next to a Salvator Mundi much taller than me.

You wouldn't be confusing me with him.

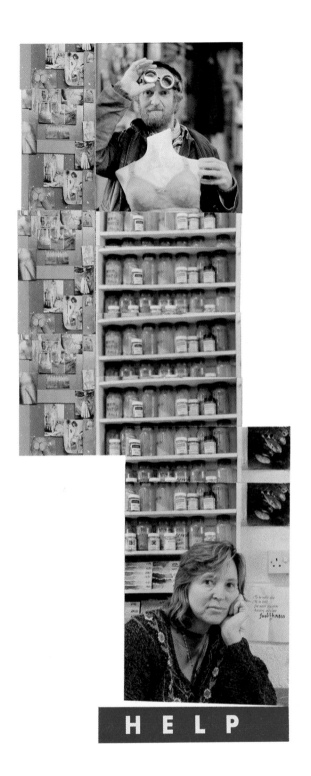

Ian and Lyn Wright have planted over two thousand trees, and made habitats for plants, bugs and critters. They have made ceramics, sculpture, concrete boats, and recently organized an exhibition called The Value of Rubbish. *Ian did most of the talking.*

The best of the End

People said how brave we were to leave England, I can't work out why. I remember being introduced once at a party: 'This is Ian, who lives like other people wish they could.' These days I just look at people and think, Why aren't you worried about the state of the planet? Every tree knocked is a knell, a nail in the planetary coffin. Lyn and I are split on this one: If things got bad I'd be out there milking the irradiated cows; whereas Lyn would take a pill. When I was in my teens I used to imagine horrendous scenarios of what was going to happen to us. Trying to find an optimism meant you learned to survive: to milk cows, clean pigs, make butter, grab a bit of life before the whole thing collapsed, make the best of the End.

When we stopped making ceramics we realized what we've got that most people haven't got, and that is a headful of ideas. 'I've got a headful of ideas and it's driving me insane.' It took us thirty-odd years to realize most people haven't got any ideas. I used to get very daunted by well-bred people and I still have a bit of a job there, I still feel, Oh God, I haven't got a very good education, and, oh God, I'm only that tall, only a little student. And then they happen to mention that the car's on lease and they've got a second mortgage and you think, Who's right and who's wrong?

We own this property and we can go off to Africa for three months of the year, so we're not doing too badly. But I have to remind myself, because the rest of the world out there are reminding me the opposite: get into debt, get into business. When we stoped doing ceramics everybody said, But why? Haven't you got orders? Yes. Well, set up a factory, borrow some money, they said. It's hard not to be influenced, not to be trapped.

The worst line of all when you give someone the bill is that they say, 'But you enjoyed doing it, didn't you? You can't charge that much for something you enjoy.' As if you always had to suffer to earn money. The only reason I'd like to win the lottery is so that I could buy a lot of land so that the farmers wouldn't fuck it up. Businessmen talk about taking risks – with money, to make more money. We take different kinds of risks. We stop doing one thing and we start another. It gets to the point where you just don't get up in the morning, where you're so unmotivated by what you're doing. You've just got to do something about it. And to do that you have to have freedom in your head.

You don't get ideas sitting in an office trying to get ideas. You've got to have a gestation period. You can't design a table in a week, or if you do, the table you create isn't a conclusion, it hasn't flowed. Rubbish or concrete boats or sculptures aren't that different. You're working out ways of using materials, using an idea: like a light bulb translated into an oil lamp, a number-plate into a saucepan. Expats in Africa drive past these things for twenty years and never see them.

I realized when we started going to Africa that I'm good at coping with African politics. I seem to communicate better with people out there than I've ever done here. The rubbish exhibition just evolved, like most of the things we've done here. I had no idea that showing African rubbish would be the way of getting through to people in Ireland. I'm really pleased with that. I haven't got the kind of head that would have predicted how much easier it would be to teach through the example of other people's rubbish. Though of course it's not rubbish to Africans, it's a necessity of life. Quite different from recycling in our society. You happen to have got a number-plate and you need a saucepan. And they have an innate aesthetic sense – that hasn't been crushed.

I've always been fascinated by what's going wrong with education. People are losing their aesthetics and their skills. It's hard to believe that could be educated out. I learned a lot from those people in Africa. Much more than I learned in college! Another thing you have to learn is letting go. The exhibition is touring around and it's out of my hands now. The concrete boat project is like that too. I just needed to be an irritant in the system for a while and get it going. Then I'm free to work on water-purifying systems – and home-made windmills are going to be my next one.

It's an incredible juggling act, between having ideas and carrying them out. You're on the phone to someone and you have to explain that all the balls aren't in the air at the moment. Every so often you lose it and more and more of them are falling to the ground all over the place. And that's when I come back to planting trees. Planting two thousand trees in the grand scheme of things is very little, but when people come in and see what you've done and then go and plant up forty-acre farms, you realize your two thousand trees are responsible for that.

the best of the end

Lily van Oost lived for many years in the Black Valley of County Kerry, working as an artist, sculptor and weaver. She also wrote a thousand-page autobiography called The Liliad. *A few weeks after we met her, and following what she had described as her very exciting fight with cancer, she died.*

Black and white

I wake up at three or four o'clock in the morning and I get up and I work. At eight o'clock I feel a bit tired. My dog hears me scraping my pen, and going tick tick tick to wash it a bit. He stands there waggling his tail and thinks, There's a chance of going for a walk if I play my cards right. So I go for a walk with him. If I have been shopping, I have to cook for a week. I don't understand why people have to go shopping every day. So I shop once a month and cook once a week, or once every two weeks. Things accumulate in the deep freeze, and around eight o'clock in the morning I have to decide what I shall I take out to have it defrost by supper time.

I am supposed to have dinner, but I am too tired, so I fall asleep and then wake up again and walk the dog or not walk the dog depending on what's calling me. Normally at five o'clock I'm dead, I'm snoring. I wake up a couple of hours later; even sometimes half an hour later I'm all alive and kicking again. Very deep sleep – which is very healthy. I don't even hear the telephone beside me. I don't hear knocking at the door. I don't hear anything. Then I work again after that. So it's working, walking the dog, sleeping, and working in the garden is my hobby. I have shrubs, and a lot of chickens. You feed them around the shrubs and they scratch and scratch, they do your gardening. And off you go again working. If there is something political you want to follow on the radio, you turn it on. And you can turn it off, but if you turn it off, the dog thinks he's going for a walk!

If you want to go to the bathroom here, there are no walls, and I know there is someone in there if the door is closed. It is the same with my life, there are no walls, and one door. All thoughts, all vibrations can come in and out, and I have a door that I close very well. That's how I got here. I was a black sheep in the family, and it was easy for me to make a decision. Where I grew up, the posh families educated their children in French, but I had only the right to talk Flemish with the maid. She had big tits that I was allowed to caress! Behind my parents' back. Everything was always behind my parents' back. My father was an uncivil engineer, my mother was the lady of the house. I was the oldest one so I was the experiment.

I grew up saying no to everything. Being a black sheep it's easy to say no. The real black sheep in the field are very nice, but being rejected as a human being is pretty horrible. I went to school when I was two and a half, and I started drawing and drawing. And I loved theatre. I wanted to become a ballerina, a ship's captain on the high seas, a chemist, and a sculptor. All of those things. I have done things for theatre. I have been dancing a lot – mostly when I had a few too many. As for chemistry, I was mixing colours. As for the captain on the high seas – if you look out here, this house is like a ship. This house is like a ship full of plants.

The stuff I was really born to and born for is drawing, mostly black and white, because it's the most difficult stuff. The nibs are so small, but you can do the biggest things with them. The artist needs a high-quality brain. A lot of people think being an artist is a very vague thing, that the artist just has to say, I have this message to the world, or, I haven't found myself yet, I am looking for myself, where am I? You have been sitting on that same ass for years, and you still have to find yourself!

I married when I was quite young. The big escape. I started practising at seventeen, and then my father caught me and said, It's too late now to turn back. I knew the marriage would be a failure. My husband didn't want children – he was a pink-assed accountant. Money money money. I really wanted children and I got two, but bloody hell, what a job! You want to be the best mother in the world and there is no perfection. It's like making the best painting in the world, there's no such thing. So I was a very bad mother – and I was the best one. I didn't give them what I didn't want when I was a child – a gagging order, plaster over your mouth and cotton wool in your ears, silence when you eat. I hated that. My children I gave bloody freedom and they reproached me! They didn't want to be artists. They didn't like my *joie de vivre*. They were embarrassed. It was impossible. I loved my children and I'm sure they loved me, but they were bossing me. The youngest one never wanted to eat anything I prepared. She wouldn't eat *foie gras* on toast or caviar with cauliflower! I loved spaghetti, I ate spaghetti every day.

So my marriage was a catastrophe. I had saved some money from drawings and paintings I had sold – my husband didn't know I'd hidden it. I bought this house with that money. I felt like a dog let free after years of being jailed. A big dog living in a small apartment going to live in the countryside. I came first to Ireland with another young woman. We hired a car together and travelled Ireland. I was thirty-five. I fell in love with Ireland on the ferry in Liverpool. I saw the *sans-gêne*, the couldn't-care-less attitude, there was no problem at all with having holes in your clothes. Two years later I came with another friend and we did the tour. Clonakilty, Puck Fair, Mayo and up north. We came back here, went to Kate Kearney's cottage and then we walked, and we stopped at the top of the Gap, and I painted. That same night I had had a dream about a house and it looked exactly like this one, but the sky was green and the grass was blue, which was strange.

The next day we were at the waterfall, and I was washing myself, and there comes this sheep farmer, and he'd just inherited this house with one acre. I said, Is there anything for sale? because I was beginning to think, I love this country so much. I felt like I had been here before, in the valley. I know that's rubbish. I don't believe in second and third lives. I just felt at home here. Ten minutes later I had the key in my hand. That was that.

I couldn't come and live here because the children weren't old enough yet. But then they got their boyfriends, they had steady relationships, they were happy. So I came here and I was painting and painting. I won't speak about my sex life, it would take till next year. I always said I will never die regretting what I have done, I might die regretting things I have not done. That would be a pity, so I'd better do them. I had no shame, no shame at all. I believe that sexuality is a fantastic thing, very good for your mind. It releases your energy so well into your work.

I knew I was going to have a very hard time financially. I never make a concession. Fishes on dishes and flowers in vases and women draped on

black and white

a cushion, and a cat on a rat, no thanks very much. I had a class for children, which was interesting for a few years, but it gets very boring in the end. For several years, once a year, I have tried to make money going to the craft trade fair, but it's all the worse for my reputation, because they're asking, are you the artist who makes pullovers? I say yes, socks as well. An artist doesn't make pullovers. I'm very good at saving money also. I wasn't going to pubs any more. I don't smoke, I don't use drugs. I can live very cheaply. I make my own clothes. I grow some of my own food. I'm not demanding about food, just some healthy stuff, and spaghetti!

You have to have a rich life with you before you start living in a place like this, a full life, full of poverty, full of anything as long as it's rich. You have to have read a lot. I go religiously to a book instead of to a church. Then you have the radio. And I get a weekly newspaper. I said before this is like living in a ship, without a crew, but there are plenty of fishes around! When you have your head so full, so full of visions ready to burst out, it's like being a volcano full of lava, or should I say, like a colon full of shit! When you're bursting like this, you cannot live with anybody else. It's simply not possible, not viable. Nobody can live with me.

An artist has the gift of translating the invisible into the visible, and what you think into what you see. An artist is a transmitter in need of an aerial. A good aerial is an aerial which is well-serviced. That is your responsibility. If I start drinking every day, if I start smoking every day, I have no money. Every packet of cigarettes is that much ink, that much drawing paper gone. If I start drinking it's my liver that goes, my brains. If I live in a place, like a town street, I lose my time talking, I get blurred and my aerial is useless. That is also why I live here, out of the way of all these things.

Not everybody can live in a place like this, but what I can't believe is that you can live without having your ears open, never mind your eyes. It is incredible. Do you know how many people are living in the republic of China? Do you know how many people there are in the world? My doctor doesn't know. And that's a scandal. There are one billion two hundred million people in China, and there are five billion people on this earth. That's more than a fifth. Me – is nothing. My house – is nothing. At the moment, on this earth, there are as many people living as there were from the appearance of humanity till today. I find that absolutely fascinating; it refreshes your mind and gives you a shock.

I stopped working on *The Liliad* when I discovered I had cancer. It was an autobiography, from day one, me lying with a naked bum and some lacey hat, on white sheepskin of all things, and I was even looking appetizing. Sleeping beauty. *The Liliad* was about black sheep, and the war, and the size of the moon and the millions in China. That's what I felt should come out. And then I got so ill. So that was another fight. I had a choice – am I editing? am I having exhibitions? am I fighting my ill-health? – because of course without health you can't stay alive, and if you can't stay alive you can't work. So I decided I would do the two last things: to stay alive to work. Work is the most important thing to me. There's no decision. There's nothing else existing. It's true.

We cannot take life for granted, can we? I may be cut to be pieces by a car when I step out of here. Even worse, by a lorry! There are some days when I'm depressed. Meanwhile it's just black and white. I think it's the closest to the truth. I don't try to be like that. I've always led a very colourful life, to say the least.

At Mount Melleray, a Cistercian monastery in County Waterford, hundreds of years of silence can still be felt. The Cistercians were founded in 1098, in France. 'The French have very good monks,' says Father Kevin, 'they have a tradition of thought and contemplation. Here in Ireland we like to talk.'

Silence

We grew up in Clonmel, up the road from here, and my brother John used to say to me, 'Those monks up there, they get up at half past one or two, they never eat meat, they use sign language, they work in the fields and they give their life to God and to prayer.' That was the first I heard of Mount Melleray. I liked a certain amount of silence and being on my own. When I was about twenty and went to parties, I was never happy, I always wanted to get just one person in a corner and talk and talk and talk. I don't like chit-chat. At the time, life was like an orange with all the juice gone. I felt that by coming to Mount Melleray I was going to make up for the wasted part of my life. I was hopping from here to there, putting down roots nowhere. I'd been to university and didn't finish; I worked in a big firm for a while; then my aunt died and gave me a business, which I didn't want. I didn't really know what I wanted, but I knew something was missing. I came up here to give this a try and it worked – here I am.

When I entered there were about a hundred and thirty monks, and thirty or forty of those would have been under thirty years of age. Now there are forty-seven and most of them are old. The average age is sixty-six. There's no appearance yet of an upturn. There will be one, but it's not going to come for some time. It would have to be an intervention of God. When I talk to someone who wants to be a novice, I ask myself, is this just some idea he's got or is it coming from God? Has he a quiet, contemplative temperament that's able to cope with a lot of monotony? You have to have some gift for it. It takes a long time to tell whether or not people can cope with the solitude. We send people for psychological testing. It's a difficult life, we wouldn't want people to get stuck in it. It's like getting married to the wrong person. Quite a lot have left after twenty or twenty-five years. Initially they stay here by force of will, and then they start to break up psychologically. God wouldn't call anyone to a life of peace when they had no peace. I have peace. I have no big problem with things. I've said to people sometimes that there's *nothing* they could bring me that I want, and they can hardly believe me.

St Benedict wisely said that the only way to be a successful hermit is first to live in a community. We all have our own little jobs to do in the community, but if there's a community job we must forget our own needs and join in. The three things around which our lives revolve are prayer, work and *lectio* – that's meditative reading – about an even proportion of each. Everybody needs discipline. There's a beauty in it, even if you can't see it at the time. The first monks went out to the desert to get away from the decadence of Christianity. From the beginning, monasticism was a reaction against society. It arose when, following great persecution of Christians, a harmony was established between church and state, and people flocked into the church in thousands and thousands, with the result that standards went down. You only have high standards when there's an élite. Cistercians built walls around their monasteries, whereas Dominicans and Franciscans often had schools for the parish. With the Reformation, monastaries almost faded away. Mount Melleray is the first post-Reformation monastery in Ireland. We had almost forty houses in this little country. Five houses now.

Cistercians still keep within their walls as much as they can. When I first came here you could only see your family a few times a year, and had to have special permission to see others; whereas now we see people more often, and we do more for people who want to come here on retreat. We're a more noisy community since speech came in 1972. I preferred sign-language, it can be very expressive. A bigger change, the same year as silence went, was the end of the distinction between lay brothers and choir brothers. If you had your secondary education you became a choir brother, and otherwise you became a lay brother. That was all right in medieval times, when most people couldn't read and write. It was very unfair to have lay brothers in our times, who wore brown habits rather than black and white, and didn't have any say in the running of the place. It was quite hierarchical. Long ago the abbot sat on a throne. Since Vatican II we're all called people of God, in an attempt to get away from that hierarchical thinking – Jesus was one of the common people. But a community needs a leader. Obedience is very important in our life. You can't be disagreeing with the abbot.

Monastic life will always mirror the world outside. There's a lot of freedom outside now, so people inside are also looking for more freedom. We get newspapers, and listen to the radio to a certain extent. But when I see my own nephews, I know they wouldn't fit into a life in which you go to bed at the same time, get up at the same time, always. I would prefer the monastery to come to an end rather than start off something new. This life is structured in a certain way for certain ends; if it changes, you can't attain the end, I think. We need time to be with God, to become the person God wanted us to become. The earlier we get up the more we keep the world away from us. If we start getting up at seven or eight, people can come here all the day, and that wouldn't do at all. Night-time is always the time of prayer; when there's stillness, no tractors, people are quiet and there's a quietness in ourselves. If we had a discussion in the community and decided to start getting up late, then I'd leave. I didn't come here for that. I came here for a special reason. If we've something to offer it's because our lives are different.

Monks know how to observe things, to listen to the wind, watch the sun rise, listen to birds singing, watch the moon on the grass. I was lucky as a little kid, that I was touched by beauty. Most people outside would think you were mad, enjoying these things at 6 o'clock in the morning. People who buy four or five newspapers on a Sunday, and sit back and watch the television, they wouldn't like it here. We want to quieten down our lives, and observe things. You get a great sense of peace being near people who are quiet, you plug into their psychological system and you become quiet when you're near them. And then there are others who plug into you, and you go away drained.

I think too that when good people live together – and their buildings, walks, trees – they all have a certain aura which would be the opposite of a haunted house. Rationally you can't explain it, but there's a great

silence

peace in certain places. People who work on the farm here, they often have transistors on, and they're not even listening, they can't hear them. God gave us five senses and they must be alert. Today's world deadens your senses, we must try and sharpen them. Walking in the mountains here you can feel human love; you can reach the point when you don't need to talk. God is an absentee landlord at times, but in silence, something does happen. Your soul is touched. You can't explain it in human terms. You cry, not tears of sorrow, tears of joy.

Father Denis became a novice five years ago.

I'd been coming here for a long time, as a place to get away. For about two or three years before I came I had it in the back of my mind, but I was just too busy, working in an office in Dublin. I was very happy at it, as far as I knew, but I always kept up the contact here. It came on me gradually that it was something I wanted. It seemed worth the price. There was the attraction of prayer, the challenge of living a life of love in one place.

A lot of the older people can remember days when there were two hundred people here. But the figures are artificial in a way; they don't relate necessarily to vocation, but to poverty and how society was. Coming here was a step up socially; now it's a step out. I didn't come here hoping it would be a large community, or that there'd be younger people, but I am aware of the numbers now – I haven't been here five years and the numbers have dropped by twenty.

I don't have any problem getting up early. I wouldn't want to change that. But, without destroying the silence and the solitude, I would like see a bit more intimacy and sharing within the group. The structure ensures a lot of silence between us. There's silence from eight o'clock in the evening to eight o'clock in the morning. In general during the day the idea is that you speak when you need to, but that it wouldn't be frivolous speech. We don't discuss things as much as I'd like. Because of the old structure of complete silence and not sharing, many of the older people are just not able for that at all. We hold series of community meetings now and then, but I often come away feeling disappointed.

Some of my friends in Dublin were stunned when I decided to come here. A few closer friends had seen it coming. I was surprised how well some of them took it. I didn't think people would see it as a valid way of life. People who come here are affected by the place in different ways. Some people get very nervous and upset, even. My brother-in-law, for example, he can't stay here at all. He leaves my sister here and goes off for a drive. He just can't stand the atmsophere. Maybe it's a fear of being on his own.

I can feel the danger sometimes of losing contact with the real world; it's very easy to get caught up in abstract ideas about why things are going on without experiencing the reality of it. I wouldn't have any ambition to change the world; it isn't the aim of monastic life and I'm glad it isn't. One of the attractions of coming here in the first place was stepping out of the business of affecting the world. I've always been wary of being effective!

We're lucky here, we're a big house and we're quite well off. We have a dairy farm, which carries the place. We employ about twelve people, some of them on the farm. I'd like to get into more food production. The fact is now that it's cheaper to buy than to grow. It was part of my own idea coming here that I wanted to work on the land. I'd be very upset if I was taken off the farm. I'd like to set up some sort of cheese production, even if it never went further than just making it for ourselves. The abbot is interested, but a change like that would be very slow to happen.

American monks take guests into choir; I like the idea of that. There'd be an objection in a lot of houses to having women inside the cloister, but that's changing too. You have to strike a balance though. I know of some monasteries, Kylemore for instance, that have been turned into tourist attractions, and the monastic element is slipping. But whether we like it or not we are a tourist attraction. In the summer it's packed out here. The car park is full of cars and buses. Over the last few years there have been people coming along who cause a certain amount of trouble. We keep a record of guests, and some might not be let in again. I feel strongly about that; people who have been coming here for a long time would be very disappointed to find that there isn't the peace they expected. It's hard to know what to do. Those people are obviously fairly desperate; they might not find acceptance anywhere else. There has to be some way of catering for all types. But there are still the faithful, people who have a purpose and want to live the life as closely as they can to the way we live it, and the more radically unlike their usual life, the better.

silence

Patrick Lydon and his wife Gladys, with their three children, plus co-workers from Hungary, France, Germany and North America, look after a dozen or so handicapped children at the Camphill community in County Kilkenny.

One black beetle knows another

If you want a model for a community, where do you look? Around you. We're in the countryside, all our our neighbours are farmers. We'd been asked to create a Camphill community for children with autism, psychosis, behaviour disturbance, and multiple disabilities. We decided to establish a community in which the farmyard would be right in the middle of the place. The children don't spend much time doing farm activities, though they do help – we all pick potatoes together, we make hay. The model for a lot of newer communities is more like a leisure centure – with swimming pool, basketball courts, and so on. The model here is a farm. Rudolf Steiner's thought is important, but it isn't the model; he was speaking about the structure of Europe, the relations of millions of people in nation states overcomimg the problems of government. At Camphill, the ideas are applied to small numbers of people living under the same roof. The inspiration is still his: a sense of freedom in most things, equality in social and economic relationships, access to things, sharing work. It was one of Steiner's followers, Karl König, who started the Camphill communities. The first was in Scotland – eleven people living in the middle of nowhere. Now it's a thriving community.

For me the path was very clear. I was a modern young American, Irish Catholic from Boston. JFK was elected when I was ten, and it was my not-so-deeply concealed ambition to be president. If you take a poll of ten-year-old American boys, 25 per cent of them expect to be president. In my last year at school I read *The Brothers Karamazov*, and it turned my mind around completely. I was particularly attached to the character of Alyosha, and the Russian monk, Zosima, and the story of the Grand Inquisitor, and the inward aspect of the story. To be president of the United States is grand, but what is that on the inside?

Those years, from reading *The Brothers Karamazov* in '68, to '72, were years of deep alienation – experiencing yourself as not part of things, or opposed to things. I was at Woodstock, and it was as amazing as anyone ever said it was, if not more so. There was Hendrix playing 'The Star-Spangled Banner' – I'll never forget it – in this infinitely alienated way, proclaiming that what was happening here could only happen in America, the land of the free and home of the brave; while in Vietnam there were bombs bursting in the air and people screaming …

I went to Yale for two years, spent a year in England, and when I went back to university I decided I wouldn't continue for four years. If you go to Yale for four years it's a very, very, powerful stream to be in – it's like being plugged into the mains. I was headed for journalism. You can't withstand Yale for four years and not think that *The New York Times* is where you have to end up. But I had a picture of a way of life, where work wouldn't be separated from my family living, and the values of family life would be connected to my work. You had to step radically out of things to even seek that way of life. When I was in England I visited Ireland several times, and I saw this was a place that was more accessible than mainstream east-coast America. Ireland was in a very different stage of evolution. I came here for a year and then decided I'd stay.

The first year I was here I heard about a priest called Father McDyer, who was a very creative thinker in a parish which had suffered serious rural depopulation, and had tried to establish various co-operatives to make local enterprise viable. I went to see him, intending to volunteer for one of those projects, and when I got there he had moved. The next morning I met a Buddhist – along the road! – from California, who was looking for land to establish a market garden, and I thought, This is the kind of thing I'd like to do. I asked him how had he learned to do that, and he said at the Camphill in Yorkshire. He said, It's a very good place to learn because they have everything – cows and tractors and so on – and they're true believers; they believe what they believe, it's not just a community where everybody comes and does their own thing. Maybe you believe in what they believe in and maybe you don't.

And that was on the Tuesday of Holy Week in 1972. I wondered would I be shell-shocked living in the countryside, with more cows than people? I was in Kerry, in Dunquin. I walked up Mount Brandon and I just realized it would be possible. Then I saw a picture in *The Sunday Independent* of people setting up a Camphill community at Duffcarrig. This was the complete fulfilment of the picture I'd imagined – but with a lot of things I hadn't imagined. The idea of community hadn't occurred to me, and I had no experience of people with disabilities. I spent two years at Duffcarrig. From the very start I knew this was it. I liked the community, and I liked caring for people. I couldn't really say I had carved out this way of life, but it all fell into place in a most fortunate way. It was a very, very powerful experience.

To live in a place where the whole idea was to build up your relations to others and to identify what you're doing and the place where you are and the people you're doing it with, rather than to step back more and more; to mean what you say and mean what you do; to build yourself up so that you are in the middle of yourself, rather than standing apart from yourself, or being somewhere else or being somebody else altogether – that was an amazing experience for me. Having known what it felt like to be outside was invaluable to me in understanding others. Though in another way, people with disabilities are very much themselves; they are where they are and they're in the middle of it, not outside it.

When I was first here, talking to farmers in the neighbourhood about setting up a community farm, where I wouldn't own the land, and wouldn't be paid, they just looked at me blankly. It was incomprehensible to them. For me, it's a great relief not to be in the mainstream of money. It's such a different possibility, a different plane. I've never drawn the dole, I've never paid tax, and I've never drawn a grant. Nowhere in the whole world is my spending recorded. Praise the Lord I'm out of it! I'm very, very happy with my financial situation. One of the concepts behind Camphill is that the less you see yourself earning your own keep, and the more you see yourself as producing wealth for the common good, the healthier the society. That is so deeply opposed to a capitalist way of thinking, or a work

one black beetle knows another

ethic. If you live beside a person who is not able to compete and work, there's no question of whether they deserve three meals a day or a dry bed, there's no issue. It changes your perspective in a very profound way. To work for their good, without the issue of knocking out your own living, is a learning process.

As you can see, I'm a born optimist, so I fall over my optimism all the time!

Noel Spence and his twin brother Roy gave up jobs as teachers about ten years ago. Noel converted a henhouse in his garden into a replica of a fifties cinema, using egg boxes for insulation in the projection room. He also writes poetry, much of it in celebration of the fifties. He lives in County Down.

Luxury Viewing Theatre

I remember my bro and I buying a battery-operated projector when we were kids and lying on the bunk bed shining it on the ceiling. It was always a fascination, showing pictures. I remember the projectionist at the old cinema in Comber would throw away cuttings and we used to bring them home, hold them up and shine torches through them and you had a picture. There was a magic in that, which video doesn't have. You can't look at it and see pictures, you can't hold it up to the light.

We were born in Comber. I moved a bit out from the village in 1974, and there was an old henhouse here, so I converted that into a cinema. I got seats from Belfast, but they got a bit shabby and worn, so I got the ones from the old Comber cinema, like a tribute.

I don't run my cinema as a business. Nobody wants to see the films I show! It's just a small select group we call the Chowder Club; we meet every Sunday evening. We've had some interesting people visiting the cinema, like Boris Karloff's daughter; and Ray Harryhausen, who brought with him the models he'd made for *One Thousand Years BC.* I was projecting the film, and I could see down there on the stage the models, and on the screen was the film in which he'd used them, and sitting there in the front row the bald head of the man who had made them. I was looking through the porthole in the projection room, and it was a privileged, magical moment.

When I was teaching, I kept the two parts of my life totally separate. When I left teaching there weren't two parts to my life any more. I suppose you could call it a mid-life crisis. I was about forty, and I was thinking: I've gone about as far as I want to go with teaching. My brother was vice-principal in another school, hacking his way up. Life was so cramped, so regimented; people would always know exactly where I was, what building I was in, what room at what hour. It's an irrational fear of not being able to cope, or provide, or guilt at letting the family down, that makes people stay in jobs they don't like. But the truth is that families don't care. They're not a bit grateful. When I was teaching I realized I wasn't enjoying the summer holidays either. I'd get off on the thirtieth of June and by the end of the first of July I'd be saying to myself: There's one day gone. So I knew there was something wrong. For me to go on teaching would have been like a minister going on preaching after he'd stopped believing in God. There's this myth that if you educate everybody you make a better society, but you only make people more dissatisfied, more assertive and more belligerent.

But we've had great fun since, my brother and I. The first thing we did after we gave up teaching was making Christmas grottoes for big stores. In our heyday, about two years ago, we were doing grottoes all across the province. Now we do more video production – promotional work for con artists selling double glazing, or whatever nonsense. Four of the five companies we've done videos for have gone bust, so there must be a message there! They seek us out, these companies. The lemming principle. We never advertise. You can see why! But seriously, we get work by word of mouth. All sorts of work. Anything that's play. I have a Catholic friend who goes on retreat. But I like to think my whole life is a retreat. It's fun.

What did George Bernard Shaw say? Happy is a man who can make a living from his hobby. Roy and I never do anything we don't want to do. We're never going to be wealthy, but we're not starving and we're not freezing. When I left that job – which was regarded as a plum job, I was senior English teacher in an élite girls' school – there was a queue from here to Enniskerry and back of people wanting it. Everybody thought I'd gone off the rails. Some of the people I used to work with regard me still with a mixture of resentment and hostility. And some of them to this day believe that I won the pools. They can't believe anyone would do something like that. If I did win the pools I'd probably still eat the same breakfast, sleep in the same bed. There's no aspect of my life I want to change. You know those catalogues that big stores have, I can go through them cover to cover and there's absolutely nothing I want. You hear people saying, I must go through this catalogue and see is there anything I need. If they needed it they wouldn't need a book to tell them what it was.

My interest and my brother's is in the fifties. Our tastes are un-ashamedly vulgar. We like anything that's cheap and American and loud and brassy and tasteless: Formica, art deco, the plastics, and the old Dansette record player. I had an internationally known collection of old movie posters – horror, science fiction, fantasy – which was stolen in 1994. Thirty-five years of collecting. It was a priceless, beautiful, lovely collection. If I won ten million pounds tomorrow I could never replace it. My brother has got a jukebox collection – he's got nineteen or twenty juke-boxes from the fifties, those lovely, big, bubbling things.

There's a great speech in the Vincent Price film *The Fly*, in which a girl says she's afraid of the speed at which things are changing, how science is progressing so much. I share those feelings. I'd rather time had stopped in 1959. Everything was mechanical then. If the jukebox didn't work, there was always a chance you could fix it. The fifties was an age of innocence. Girls walked hand in hand. The café with the jukebox in Comber, when somebody put money in, everybody stood up and sang along with the song. It wouldn't happen today. It may seem like a small thing, but to me it represents a big change. There's a hardness I recoil from now. The buzz words are future, and new. A phrase I hate is, 'The way forward'. As if we're all standing still or going back. People are always saying to you: Now your problem is … As if you have to have a problem.

Roy and I are schoolboys, we're always looking for the easy laugh. At the most serious moments I always have some sort of irreverent thought, a sense of the absurdity of it. Someone with that kind of mentality is never destined to occupy top office. You wouldn't want your surgeon to sudden-ly see the ludicrous side when he's performing an operation on your heart. So it's as well there are a few who are serious. Sometimes I wonder are there going to be enough people to do the really important things. I think peo-ple deserve rewards for simply hanging in there, being there every day. We're fortunate that they have that sheer dogged insistence just to be there. We should maybe offer up a short prayer.

luxury viewing theatre

In 1974 Mary and Richard Douthwaite bought thirty acres of hillside near Westport, planted it with trees and built a house. Mary did the block work and the painting, Richard mixed the cement and did the carpentry. Mary works sometimes as an occupational therapist. Richard is a freelance journalist and has published two books, The Growth Illusion *and* Short Circuit.

A thousand-year horizon

Mary

It was my idea to come here. I was always going to come back. My father never stopped talking about Ireland when I was growing up. He was a regular hard-drinking Catholic, an exile, an officer in the British army. My mother was an Irish Presbyterian.

Richard and I were in the West Indies, on Montserrat, for a few years before we came here. Richard was a government economist there. We lived in a wonderful old plantation house there which is now destroyed by the volcano! This was the early seventies, but the whole thing was very Somerset Maugham. There was still a governor-general who wore white plumes. And Prince Charles came in his gunboat and we had to go and have cocktails on board. That job in Montserrat was the only regular job we ever had. I had to set to and make myself dresses, because all the cocktail set ever did was sit round swimming pools. We had these terrible coffee mornings, and it was mentioned at one of these that we'd caused problems by paying our maid Alice too much. We used to call her our technical assistant.

I had my daughter when we were out there, so I had a baby I could actually spend time with, and I sat there and dreamed of what we were going to do next. We wanted to go somewhere temperate. We didn't like the tropics. We wanted to grow stuff. We'd read John Seymour's books about self-sufficiency. So there we were in this terrible hot climate, imagining Ireland, and how we'd get up ever so early every morning and do lots of work before breakfast.

And we did. We worked all day, we didn't ever sit down. We literally didn't have chairs for a long time. You want to talk to our kids. The second one, who went to school here, wanted everything to be normal. He once saw me in town in my wellies! That was a terrible sin. I wasn't allowed to say hallo to him in the street at one stage, I embarrassed him so much. But then when he left school he thanked us for giving him such a tough upbringing, because from then on everything was going to seem easy.

I loved building the house and planting the trees. I don't seem to have a burning ambition to be doing something of my own. I think my ambition is the bit of land, the trees, and producing food. I like having a house and a garden and a family in it. And it's lovely to have this place now, for the kids, because I know they'll look after it. The only part we both hated was the business.

We made leather kits for occupational therapy. There used to be a shoe factory near here, and I discovered that they were taking bags of leather scraps down to the dump, so we decided we'd do something with that. But I was trained as a carer, not as a business person. If someone who owed us money rang up with a sob story, we'd say, that's fine. You can't run a business like that. And the day-to-day boredom and pettiness, and the banks – they're awful. The plan was always to get it started, run it for a few years to make a bit of money so we could get on with building the house, and then get rid of it. But it was the wrong time, and we were stuck with it for longer than we wanted. But it taught us both so much. A disaster does make you see.

We were going to be self-sufficient when we came here, but we discovered you can't be. Or only partially. It wasn't that we opted out, we never gave anything up – except we decided Richard wasn't going to carry on being an economic advisor and having a proper salary. Before the West Indies, we'd lived on a boat, in Oxford, in Ramsgate, and then in Wivenhoe, when Richard was at university. Starting off living on a boat and having a couple of kids meant we were living a really odd lifestyle by other people's standards.

I was supposed to go to university at Essex as well, but I was pregnant, and it just wasn't on. So Richard would come back in the evening and talk about the gold standard and I'd fall asleep. Most economists obviously haven't run a house, they don't seem to know the basic things about how to manage money. You have to be very single-minded to be an economist. Women tend to think about so many different things at a time. Running a household is like that. You need to know how much money you've got and how much you can spend.

Richard's parents were great when we were living on the boat. They used to arrive with a carload of goodies, stay for the day, have a look around and think, ugh, and then go home. Richard and I met when we were sixteen or seventeen, and Richard's family have always been really supportive, in everything. I think that's why he has such an optimistic attitude towards things. You'd think he would always be depressed about the economic system he thinks has had it, but he's always cheerful.

I have one brother, who tries to keep his end up. We didn't have a very satisfactory childhood at all. Drink was the problem. My dad drank, and my mum. My brother and I used to get up to wild things when the parents were drinking and fighting, and we'd be bored, in Africa and Hong Kong – because my father was in the army we were always moving around. So when I met Richard I couldn't believe this lovely family. I used to go to tea with them and they'd all sit down together, and talk. Nobody shouted at anybody, nobody got annoyed. I was waiting, you know how you do, for something to happen, and even now Richard's mum kids me, 'It's all right, nobody's going to shout!' Richard was this lovely, big, solid person. I grabbed, and ran.

Richard

If a new type of culture is to develop anywhere in the world, rural Ireland is the place where it will probably happen. Tom Collins of Maynooth says the ideas that inspired and helped shape the foundation of the state came from the midlands, and were the product of two cultures: the Irish culture that had been driven by invaders into the west, and the Norman, British culture. It was largely people from the midlands who became the Free State's first civil servants and the politicians.

The emerging culture is in the west, where you get ideas that have been brought in by outsiders – whether they be Irish or from elsewhere –

a thousand-year horizon

fusing with the small farm, local community, way of life. In rural Ireland generally, there is a lot of social capital. A community of a thousand people has locally owned businesses, organizations like credit unions, Tidy Towns committees, doctors' surgeries, all these things. In a similar community in Britain they're probably having difficulty keeping their pub open. Places like Tallaght or Clondalkin in Dublin have no assets of their own at all. It's this richness of the social community capital that makes the west of Ireland an ideal place for a new culture to develop.

There are periodic waves of incomers. We were the tail end of one. One of the attractions of Ireland for me was that it gave me a freedom that I probably wouldn't have achieved had I remained in England. It was a different country, and you could to some extent create another identity. Your family weren't looking quite so closely at what you were doing. Also, England felt too crowded. There were too many people trying to do the same thing. I felt the system was unsustainable and could crash, so it made sense to live in a place where the ratio of population to land was relatively favourable, where you could get access to enough land to be able to survive.

Before we came here, I'd been working as a government economist in Montserrat, and I could have gone on doing that. But we had three children by then, and we didn't want them to grow up as we had. My father was a mining engineer, and we moved around a lot during my childhood, so I was sent away to school and didn't ever come to identify with any one place in England that was home. Mary hadn't grown up anywhere in particular either. We wanted our children to feel there was somewhere they came from, because we feel that the place you come from is a very important part of your identity. And so we looked for somewhere where we could buy some land, because we wanted to become much more self-reliant. We bought a thirty-acre hillside, and spent all the money we'd brought to Ireland.

When I was an economist in the West Indies, I was dissatisfied with the mainstream system, but my ideas hadn't developed enough to do anything about it. I'd always been worried about economic growth and how it can continue in a finite world. A week ago I put out a question on the Internet: Why do conventional economists ignore this? I didn't get any satisfactory answers at all. Nobody came back and said, We don't ignore it. Some people said that asking questions like this was bad for their career!

One correspondent from the Open University told me that he'd been asking this sort of question, and had wanted economists to use longer time series so that they could be more easily projected into the future, but had been given the answer that economists dealt with the short term because the future is a series of short terms!

If you have a thousand-year horizon, you have to completely change your world view. Rather than looking at the natural environment as a resource for the economic system, you have to look at the economic system as purely a sub-set of the environment. This is an equivalent change to people thinking that rather than the sun going round the earth, it was the other way about. If you accept that the economic system that we have at present, because it relies on continuous expansion, is totally unsustainable, and very damaging, then you've got to start thinking about how you might change it.

It's too soon to say how tolerant the government in this country is towards alternative systems. I'm keen to see a zero-interest building society started. Because of changes brought about as a result of Ireland's membership of the EU, it's going to be much more difficult than it would have been twenty years ago. It would be nice to think that there was something in Irish history or mentality that might make people here more open to independent thinking. The Irish have never been like the Germans, sticklers for absolute correctness, so there's a good chance that we'll be left alone to exploit niches that we find, which is of course exactly what we've got to do.

What are the characteristics of a sustainable economy? It's stable, the population isn't increasing, it doesn't depend on economic growth, on a higher value of output coming along each year in order to survive. It will be changing very slowly, if at all, it will be very suspicious of new technologies, there will be no net investment, or very little, and as a result there will be very little saving.

How can you build this sort of thing in the present world? The only way is on the basis of community economies. In a sustainable world, each part of that world will also be sustainable. Two unsustainabilities don't cancel each other out. So every community, every country has got to be itself sustainable. In other words, its inhabitants have got to be supported by systems that provide their means of survival, which you can imagine being

a thousand-year horizon

able to continue for at least a thousand years without causing environmental degradation or the exhaustion of natural resources.

If you take a thousand-year time horizon, you can't assume that it's all going to be sweetness and light. Some communities will become unsustainable, they will degrade their local environment, they will want to take over the carefully nurtured environments of neighbouring communities. Yes, it's another version of history! Every community should be able to meet its basic needs of fuel and food from its immediate area, so that it can trade with the unstable outside world out of choice rather than out of necessity. And it's got to have some way of protecting itself against unsustainable communities. Which in turn means it's got to have its own currency system. And it can't allow the movement of capital to other communities. If we have an unsustainable economy in this area, we can take away the capital that would have been needed in your community for the repair and maintenance of your capital stock as it wore out, because we can offer a higher rate of return than you can because we're unsustainable. So you've got to have barriers to the free movement of capital, you've got to have your own currency so that you don't have to trade with the outside world purely to get the means of exchange to deal with your neighbour.

One of the main drawbacks of economic thinking in general is that it's very far from the psychology of the individual. When I was studying at Essex University, I would tell Mary as much as possible about what I'd been learning during the day. So I was telling her about the basics of economics – demand curves and supply curves, and she would say, But people don't behave like that. She'd done some psychology, and I think it was this that sowed the basic dissatisfaction with economic thought in me.

People have a problem with my ideas because their lives are unsatisfactory. They get themselves into a vicious circle. To some extent this is a deliberate creation of the system. You work hard, you take a job that doesn't fully satisfy you, but you're in it for the money. Increasingly, if you're to avoid redundancy, and if you're to climb the promotional ladder, you put in extra hours. You become aware of a basic dissatisfaction with your life, but all the messages that are coming to you, from television and so on, are that these can be overcome if you get the right car, the right wife, the right house, and so on. You've just got to work harder.

Our income here is very low, but we can do virtually everything that we want to do, so we're very rich. The only thing that we would worry about, potentially, is that we've absolutely no savings. But we do have what a lot of people don't have. The only real protection that you've got for old age is family and friends. We can count on these. In the future it may not be possible to count on the state or on commercial pension companies. You've got to be able to count on your family and your community. This is the way it's always been, and I think it's the only safe way.

John Seymour's vision of self-sufficiency was built around the nuclear family, but it doesn't make a lot of sense for husband, wife and *n* children to attempt to do everything for themselves. So while we have kept all sorts of animals here, we don't have any animals at the moment because that's better done at a community level. Some version of living on the land could work for lots more people, but many lack confidence in their skills. I was fortunate enough to go to a school where at the age of twelve I was taught to brick-lay! The other thing is the financial worries. Mary's been the key factor in our handling these, because she has a training that makes her employable, if necessary.

My writings have obviously been influenced by my own experiences. We've got a tremendous fear of debt, having been through that experience with the business. Living here, producing some of our food and fuel, we can manage on very much less. Writing brings in very little money, but I'm beginnning to get some consultancy work, and teaching courses. We built the house ourselves, and did things whenever there was money available. Time and money have rarely coincided. So twenty-two years after starting, it's still not finished. We moved in when there were no windows in it at all. We were living upstairs, we had a ladder going up to that floor, and the wind would just go straight through.

My big advantage is that I had, and still have, parents who are pre- pared to support me. This is what we're trying to provide for our children. A safety net. We also had a little money – £700 – from the sale of the houseboat we lived on in Oxford. That enabled us to buy the fishing boat we lived on while I was at Essex University. We sold that at a profit, which gave us money to build a small house in Jamaica, which we sold and then built another, and sold that when we left. That capital gave us the option to do something different. If you have nothing, you can't buy a piece of land. If you can buy a piece of land and put a caravan on it, then you're

a thousand-year horizon

away. You can start building quite slowly as materials become available.

Of course I would like to make my views available to a wider audience, but it's really difficult to know how to do so. How can you get the ideas across? I did stand in the 1994 European elections, for the Green Party, not because I wished to enter politics, but purely because it was an opportunity for presenting ideas which I thought oughtn't to be missed. Success for me in that election would have been to have lost by one vote! I didn't want to be an MEP. I don't think they or TDs or even governments have the power any longer to make really significant changes. The power has passed to multi-nationals and investors, and the European economy has to be run to suit these people.

The real challenge to me is to be able to demonstrate, in this community and in Mayo generally, that alternatives are viable, that you can put together a successful package of the sorts of things I talk about in *Short Circuit*. So you have some sort of banking organization, and a currency system which has legal teeth – a LETS system is not enough, it just introduces people to the idea. Interestingly, a currency system for all of rural Scotland is starting up next year. I'd like to do something along those lines in this community, and to develop other things to show that it is possible for communities to do many things for themselves, that there are alternative approaches to the problems of rural Ireland. There would be nothing more powerful than a working example. There's a lot of interest in eco-villages at present. They're fine as research labs, but the acid test comes when you try and do something in a historic community, working with the people you find there.

Joe Comerford has been making films since 1971. He is re-training in the new technologies in order to make a living outside film-funding agencies.

Dangerous aspirations

I went to art college because I failed the Leaving Cert and that doesn't leave you too many choices. I realized later this was a lucky occurrence. It made me look at where I was and the skills I had: I could draw a bit, so I thought I might be a commercial artist – that was the phrase then. It was around this time that my father died, my mother was ill and I crashed a car, in succession – and then I went to art college.

I was completely taken aback by the kind of questioning that was going on in college in the sixties. I felt as if everything had happened in my father's lifetime, and in my grandfather's, but not in mine. Everything had been turned upside down and then put in place, and now it was all falling apart. Trouble was building up in Northern Ireland, as well as in universities across Europe and North America. I went to America around then, and met people coming back from Vietnam – the state they were in, the mental mutilation, still gives me the shivers.

When I realized I wanted to work in film I imagined I would work in television. And I did, for a while. But it creeps up on you that what you're trying to do and what you're being asked to do have become more and more divergent. I wanted to use film as a process of discovery, as a tool, to find out information at first hand, like digging with a shovel.

There was no independent film-making at the time; nothing existed outside of television. I became a film-maker by default. One day when I was working for television I decided I was walking off the set. I was going to crack up, disintegrate. I went down to stay with friends in West Cork. Some interesting things happened while I was there. This hedge-school teacher was at the door one day, with his violin. He travelled all over the country, played the violin, talked at length; he was part of a tradition you'd associate with the last century. Such resilience, independence, formation of mind. I did learn one thing from staying in West Cork: I still wanted to make films.

One of the films I'd wanted to make for television was about addiction. There were about seven or eight heroin addicts in Dublin at the time. I went into a psychiatric hospital to work with a doctor called Noel Browne, who wanted to restore the true meaning of the word 'asylum' – a place of protection. It was a profound experience, listening to people in the hospital talk with a closeness to their emotions you seldom witness. But then you had to get on your bike and go back up to the television station and put that in some sort of format. You begin to wonder where is the real sanity.

Another example: I was working with a group of boys in Ballyfermot, and I got to know a group of travellers. I decided I wanted to make a film about travellers. I worked with somebody on the script, then did very extensive research. The BBC became involved. There was a package in place to make the film. But, the script and the production didn't really take into account getting close to these people's lives, or finding the form of the story in the subject matter and drawing it out in film; instead it was a question of developing a script separate from the subject matter, and getting actors who looked like travellers, etc.

It made me ask questions about the nature of narrative film, television productions, the process of making art. My research was giving me a connection to the travellers' lives, and, despite the fact that the production was virtually in place, I decided to pull out. I went to the west of Ireland and started from scratch. I looked for sources that would treat the film as a journey. I said to the travellers: I'm making this film, this is roughly the story, but I'm telling you now I don't know where this is going to end up – don't say I didn't tell you!

The BFI eventually went with it, and the Irish Arts Council. It was hell to make the film, but it was a very good experience. In a very unrefined way, it did extract from the subject something which many travellers had a very good and direct response to. Some audiences were completely alienated by the film, particularly here in Ireland. A lot of the subject matter has re-emerged since then: incest, rape. The perspective of the travellers was quite different on these things. It's curious that a lot of the traits that people respect in Irish culture are still found among travellers.

My grandmother set up an independent school in the thirties, and my father and my aunt taught in a similar school called Mount St Benedict, which hoped to create a questioning frame of mind in its pupils. It was closed down, in my opinion, by direct conspiracy between the Church and the new state. My film *High Boot Benny* was based on the school. 'Independence in education is a dangerous aspiration' was the inscription I put on the school's name plate.

I suppose the reason I stopped working professionally in film was the realization that there can be no such thing as an independent film – the phrase has become cringe-making. We have to find another way a film can be made as an art form in a society whose conscience is very hard to prick. However much we want to question what we're living in, part of us wants to win Oscars, have the Hollywood dream. Film is a very direct barometer of society because you have to deal with all levels of it: stock exchange, brokers, insurance, police, politicians – the core of the establishment. You have to deal with it in a dirty way, and it's getting dirtier.

We're schizophrenic about where we're going as a country; there are dilemmas that arise from the North, and at the same time we're changing from being a colonized country for centuries to being in with the colonizers. We don't ask where European money is coming from – is somebody paying for this in São Paulo?

There's a vested interest in not seeing film as an art form. Film is Hollywood to most people. Independence is a diminishing commodity – to put that on the agenda is almost impossible. Ireland is an upwardly mobile society which doesn't want to look at elements which are marginalized by that. All those people I've made films about for the last twenty-five years are more screwed now than they ever were. They're not reflected in the media. What your senses are telling you is one thing, and the media are telling you something else.

My way of dealing with it is re-training. Is technology going to redefine film? I don't know. My son is in film school, and like most young

dangerous aspirations

people he's afraid – so am I, I'm afraid all the time! It's a harsher society now. But art is the core of the reactor. People need a spiritual life, an artistic life, and a life of sustenance. The artistic life has been supplanted by notions of culture. I see a lot of culture coming out of a lot of orifices, but not a lot of art. More like manufactured consent. Is there an art of the coalface?

I use film to try and find out what's happening. I need to know, we need to know, for personal and social sanity. The more indirect the experience, the more vulnerable we are; the more direct our experience, the more sane we are. You might learn less from direct experience, but you're sure of what you know because you made the journey there. It's very hard for people to finance journeys. Half a million pounds for a journey, and you don't know where it's going! Going into the unknown could lead to something, or it may not. It's a major risk.

Chuck and Nell Kruger have lived full-time on Cape Clear since the early nineties. Among a variety of occupations, Chuck organizes an annual storytelling festival and Nell runs a craft shop. They rebuilt an old house, perhaps the southernmost in Ireland, which they rent out to visitors.

Simplify, simplify, simplify

I wanted the southernmost house to keep its sense of remoteness, and it has. People seem to love it. Lots of artists come from all over the world. It's why we came here in the first place, and why we stayed.

We left the States in 1966 because we were fed up with the Vietnam war – or 'police action', as they called it; we wanted to get away from the mentality that invents such euphemisms. I took a job as a teacher in Switzerland. We thought we were there for a couple of years, and we stayed for twenty-six. It took a lot to make us leave there. You can see what 'a lot' means. It's what you're looking at right now. We came here purely by accident – if indeed there are such things as accidents. In Elizabethan days, people had no sense of accident, everything was by design. We've lost *weltanschauung* now. Though I think there's more of it here in Ireland than anywhere else we've been.

It started back in the early spring of 1986. We'd put an option on a couple of acres of stony peninsula on Sherkin Island, and the estate agent, Ger, said to us: 'I don't know that that piece of land will ever come up for sale, but I know a piece of land which meets all your requirements, and it's much bigger and much nicer, why don't you come and look at with me? It's on Cape Clear.' So there we were on a boat to Cape Clear with Ger and his family. Nell was talking to Ger's wife, Margot, on the port side of the boat, and I was talking to Ger on the starboard side. We were swapping macho sailing stories, when all of a sudden I saw North Harbour for the first time, and I felt a rush coursing through my body from my toes to my head, and I started weeping. I had this irrational feeling: here is a place where I've got to die, where I could happily die.

Three months later I was telling this story when we had some friends round to dinner in Switzerland. Nell looks up at me and says, 'Well you never told me that, did you? I was on that same boat with you, remember, and I was talking to Margot – not just about children – and I looked at the grotto and the cemetery at North Harbour as we came in, and I had a rush of feeling that this was where I could happily die, and I wiped away a tear.' We're not lachrymose people. The power of the initial experience was extraordinary; we didn't choose this place, it chose us. I've fallen in love twice in my life, once with Nell, and once with this island, and they were both love at first sight.

I remember talking to my old analyst, and he said, Chuck, you want to beware of islands in a dream. An island is usually a symbol of a complex, and in fact it can become a psychosis. You move to an island and you're cut off from the mainland, Chuck, the mainland is where real people live! The ancient Greeks, everywhere they went they built an *omphalos* – the navel of the world, the very centre of things. This stone table I built right here is my omphalos here on the island. There have been three books written here on Cape Clear, and from each book you can tell where the person lives. Their vision has the context of the area where they are. My book is written from the South Harbour point of view. I speak from this spot, and through this spot.

This is a politically sensitive island. I made a cartoon of me and Dinnie Cadogan – he's the one who has that lovely farm over there, the one with the pentagonal fields – on either side of the harbour, each with binoculars, watching each other's every move! In a small community like this – only fifty people year-round – you are as if under a magnifying glass.

Almost everyone here – especially the ones who are over sixty-five – they all remember when storytelling was a way of life. One lovely fella, Paddy Burke, who had the excellent pub over there, said to me, Chuck, when the fella with one eye sat down in the corner, we stopped connecting with each other.

Storytelling reinstates the community. A good storyteller incorporates everything that's going on in a room, and will gear the story to the *gestalt* of the room. If there's a noise, or someone falls asleep, a knock on the door, it becomes part of a story.

I became interested in stories through being a teacher and administrator. As a teacher I became interested in stories because every once in a while I'd tell my kids stories, and I'd see that instead of putting them to sleep I'd wake them up, they'd become involved in it.

I barely know anyone here who does only one thing. There's one fishing boat left on this island. There are only three men who fish full-time. And I don't know one farmer who makes a living from farming. They all do three or four different things. And so do I. I do consulting, I write articles, I do editing, I write poems, I try to keep up the farm and the houses and do all the repairs I'm capable of doing. Nell looks after the house, and she has the craft store and makes stuff for that. It's not easy on an island. But Thoreau's motto was, Simplify, simplify, simplify. That's what we're learning how to do here. The clothes I'm wearing, they're clothes I'm wearing out. Except for socks and underwear I haven't bought any clothes since we've lived here.

You see the reek over there, the haystack, I've helped build that seven or eight of the last ten summers. Just the way things used to be. If you had a haystack to build, all your neighbours would come round and help. There was a sense of community, you're doing something constructive, something basic. Part of the value of being here is being able to do things like that. Here you have to be able to rely on yourself, have faith in yourself. You can't get on the phone and say, hey, come and fix my washing machine. It might be a month before anyone comes. You have to take much more upon yourself. Before Nell and I moved here, I asked a lot of people on the island, What advice would you give me? They all said, Learn to do things for yourself. So now I can scythe grass, I can drive a tractor, I can back up this hill of a road. I'd never done things like that before. You have to learn new flora, new fauna. I didn't know any of the sea creatures, anything about tides or currents, let alone force-ten gales. We gave up a cost of living in Switzerland for a quality of life here. It would have been unthinkable when I was in my twenties or thirties. I was a meek little fellow, afraid of my own shadow. When I came here I still had agoraphobia, I couldn't go near the edge of the cliffs. Now I'm like a mountain goat.

simplify, simplify, simplify

In some ways we've toughened up, living here, and in other ways we've become more sensitive. Almost every day I get up and look out and I can't wait to see what's different and what's the same, the light, the tides, everything is so much more exciting around me and inside me than it's ever been before. It's close to grace. I'm fifty-seven now and I feel the luckiest guy in the world. I have a little rock I call the chair up there on the headland, and when I really want to look, I go up there. And when I really need to commune I go down to a secret tunnel! This island gets bigger and bigger; the more I come to know it, the more I realize I don't know it, so I'm not getting bored.

Cape enables my life to be an adventure. Yesterday I went out in my kayak by myself, it was flat calm, and I went places where I would never allow anyone to go if I had any say about it. I saw things I've never seen before. I had porpoise coming up beside me, I had dolphins coming up beside me, I went into inlets boats can't go into. There's a cave under our farm here that goes in for two hundred metres, you really need to wear a helmet because you could be crushed by the roof. Seals pop up in there, and I don't want to come between a cow and her pup, so I've never touched the back wall of the cave, but I love going in there. I'm getting to know both sides of every wall on this island – and there are a lot of walls.

Freda Rountree runs a tree nursery in County Offaly.
She is chairperson of the Heritage Council.

The name of the weed

I was the second of five children, the second daughter. My father gave up on having a son, and took me on as his potential successor. From a very early age he brought me around with him on the tractor; I spent hours out with him ploughing and looking at earthworms, collecting them up into little heaps the way children will. He used to talk about me and my shadow, and I was his shadow.

I grew up with a very strong sense of the country and of the inhabitants of it, which farmers have lost now because, for example, you use MCPA to spray off grasslands, so none of the names of the weeds are of any importance. I grew up knowing the colloquial names of all the plants, just because they were of economic importance. You knew what they did, and that some of them were worse than others. Another thing that's lost is the names of all the fields around. I had that kind of childhood – being in contact with everything around you – and I never lost it.

In rural Ireland when I was growing up, people didn't have television and cars so entertainment was more local. There was a rambling house just across the road from here, and people used to go up there at night. After harvests when they'd have a lot of help at the house, they'd all be telling stories about particular foxes and particular badgers; as a small child you'd have your feet curled up under the table because you'd be afraid these beasts would bite you, they'd be so alive in your imagination. One was about a badger who'd got caught in one of those old vicious rat-traps; and he tramped around for years and years with this chain behind him. I heard him. I think it's probably those kinds of stories that ghosts come from.

It was AE said that the Irish are a very conservative people. They establish orthodoxies. The orthodoxy of my childhood was that improvement was a bigger house – a bungalow – modern conveniences, having money, being able to go places. I went away to boarding school, and there were girls at school talking about various desserts they'd had when they were home for the weekend, things I hadn't tasted, like Angel Delight. There was a kind of keeping up with the Joneses, a feeling that what was shop-bought was better. You certainly didn't boast about homemade even if you liked it. If something was mass-produced it was better. I think homemade is beginning to be a good word again, rather than hand-made, which is the upmarket version.

People are beginning to realize that there are an awful lot of things you don't need, like detergents, cosmetics, things that make your jumper softer, your washing whiter. They're beginning to realize that ads are selling them things they don't particularly want. It's a process people have to go through. I find it increasingly difficult to shop, because there are all sorts of things that you don't choose to buy for all sorts of reasons, and the range of food and commodities that are of value to you is very small. You can produce an increasing amount of it yourself. People are beginning to realize that they can live better with less. The process is well under way. Once 10 per cent of the population do things in a particular way, a watershed is passed. Same thing with climate: once you've got 10 per cent tree plantations on the land you affect the climate, you get higher rainfalls. We're coming up to 10 per cent in Ireland, but the wrong kind of trees – too much of one species, not enough of the ones that lead to diversity of insect and animal life.

In terms of what we find desirable in this country we seem to have gone through a process of seeking the exotic. I remember a German woman saying to me, the plants that you Irish put in your gardens we put in our cemeteries. We're developing an aesthetic that's Irish; we haven't had an aesthetic for several hundred years. The bungalow book has been responsible for a Spanish style of architecture which will become indigenous. One of the things that's gone wrong in recent times is that architects haven't been involved in the housing styles of ordinary people. Something like 95 per cent of the world's houses are not architect-designed. We need to bring the architect back into house design, and develop regional styles which carry on themes that have been there for a long time.

One thing I think is a lovely idea is that, whenever somebody builds a house, they put in something made out of local timber, whether it's a window, or a door, or furniture. People have lost that link of the usefulness of timber. When you buy timber at a timber yard you have no concept of how it got to be there. When people make the links, they also create the local jobs where you have the local furniture maker who makes the kitchen table and chairs for you. It should be more valuable, in all sorts of ways, than something you buy in the shop. The quality of hardwood we're capable of growing in this country is second to none, and we haven't even begun to realize that.

I hope I can have an influence. I like to grow things, and growing trees is the ultimate in growing things because what you grow lasts for a long time. I grew up on a tillage farm, and I worked in forestry for twenty years – sawmilling, cutting fencing posts, timber for building, garden fencing. If you combine an interest in forestry and growing up on a tillage farm, you end up growing trees. I think I was the first nursery to specialize in broadleaf trees. It was a bit of a shot in the dark at the time, but it worked out quite well. Grants for broadleaf are higher than for conifers, so it was probably a good move, though I don't plan my business in order to make money, I plan it in order to make a living. Some people say the trees I sell are too cheap; the price of them is the money I need to stay doing it next year, which is a different thing from making money out of it. I work in order to be able to work next year.

I always had a notion that if you have a job, you do something you don't particularly like to make money to do the things that you like doing. I was slow to realize that you can do the things that you like and make your living out of it. And if you do that, what do you need to make more money for? You end up in a tax bracket, for every pound you make you give seventy five pence back to somebody. There doesn't seem to be much point. The tax system in Ireland is a penal tax system. The bracket after the dole doesn't offer an incentive to earn money. If I take on labour here, all I'm doing is creating headaches for myself.

I like being solitary; I'm very good at it. I exist very well with myself.

the name of the weed

Very few people are prepared to do the kind of work I do – the kind of work people did a generation ago without thinking about it. Labour has been demeaned, there's no social status attached to it. The kinds of crafts where people worked with raw materials have died out because of the labour content – people aren't prepared to do that any more.

I love the combination of going out and doing physical work, and, if it's a wet day, coming in and doing some writing. The ability to do the two is very important to me. I think we've thrown the baby out with the bathwater in throwing aside the physical labour. The other thing I like, is if I'm regularly outside in my nursery, the birds and the wildlife get to know me, and they carry on without paying too much attention to me; whereas if someone strange comes in they'll all alarm and go off. It's very nice to feel that you're accepted as part of the natural environment.

There are some young people, and some older people, who can appreciate those things. Fewer young people have the opportunity to come into contact with the natural environment. When I was small, something like 70 per cent of the country was rural, and now 60 per cent is urban; that's a profound difference in a generation. In Ballymun, Tallaght or Cabra, people have become extra people, unemployed, like a labour store, available should it be needed; they're people who don't have a function. The waiting lists for rural resettlement show that there is a desire, and I think rural Ireland has to provide the capacity, for them to come back. Reviving traditional crafts is one way we can include people back into the rural environment.

In the heritage area we make this division between the cultural and the natural, which has no basis in fact. Humans have decided they're apart, that they come from space, but they're as natural as a rabbit or a bird. Our impact on the landscape is a natural impact, by definition, because we are natural. But we seem determined to see ourselves as something else. I sometimes wonder if it isn't a racial memory of every race having come from somewhere else?

If you look at the landscape we have now, the biggest impact has been grazing animals. People put the animals there. It's only when we realize we're part of it, a natural part of the whole, that we begin to have to take responsibility for our actions. When I was growing up, the attitude towards what grew was, Is it useful? If you could use it, it was good, if you couldn't, it was bad. We're on the point of an enormous change in our mindset about our place. Maybe the de-religionizing this country is going through is part of that. Darwin was around a long time ago, but it's only now we're beginning to treat humans as a species. We've only now begun to take ourselves down from the pedestal and look at ourselves as a species to see how we are and what we do. That's a very fruitful way of looking at ourselves, and I think it's part of the solution.

You have to relate this to the whole history of social structure. In order to have a structure, people had to have a place in the structure. They didn't necessarily need to understand why they were where they were; the most important thing was that the structure should be stable. In order to have any kind of stability on that planet, we now have to take responsibility for our own personal actions. That's the other side of the personal freedoms that people were shouting about in the sixties.

It's all a process of maturing as a species. I remember selling trees to a local farmer. He wanted something that would grow very fast and be no trouble, and I was saying to him: Put a shelter belt in, but why don't you plant inside that something which will be a bit slower growing, oaks for example? And he said: But there won't be anyone around in sixty years' time. A lot of people have in their minds the feeling that the world hasn't much further to run. That is a very frightening thing: it means they feel they can get what they like out of life because there won't be more than one generation after them. You have to put into people's minds the idea of responsibility to future generations. One of the very encouraging stories from the nursery was a man coming down to buy trees, not because he wanted to, but because he cut down trees at home and his children said, If you cut down trees you must plant some in their place. They nagged at him so much that for the sake of peace he came down to buy some trees. I think for a long time people associated big broadleaf trees with estates, and for that reason there was a generation that disliked trees. Their children have got over that one, but it's taken this long. The parklands of today are the golf courses. They're the only places with the space to put in imposing trees.

I remember one day I wanted to hang a gate, and I wanted a gatepost, and there was this old European larch which was ten yards from where I needed the post, so I said a word of thanks to whoever had planted it. That tree had been planted to be useful. They knew that they wouldn't use the tree but that somebody would. The trees I've planted here won't be of any particular benefit to me, but will be to somebody.

the name of the weed

174

Bernard Loughlin, with his wife Mary, is director of The Tyrone Guthrie Centre at Annaghmakerrig, a residence for artists and writers near Newbliss in County Monaghan.

A broad, generous and trusting wish

We had spent seven or eight years in different parts of Europe, and then we moved back to Ireland. I was teaching English as a foreign language to Saudi Arabians and Libyans, and it was getting more foreign to me by the minute. We were living in a very nice flat in a lovely area of Dublin, overlooking Palmerston Park, where you could see sparrowhawks nesting and homosexuals cottaging, and all the joys of urban life. It was one of those periods when you find yourself almost instinctively scanning the jobs ads, and then this thing swam up, as well as a job as wildlife warden in one of the national parks, which were being set up at that time. So I was applying for both simultaneously, and seeing them as in some way connected.

We came between Christmas and New Year of 1980 to have a look at the place, which was being renovated – doors off, windows off, and empty – and we immediately felt that this was it. The children were at an age when a move was possible, particularly a move to the country. We knew we liked country life, and particularly in this context, where, as a friend of mine said, it's not so much *rus in urbe*, more like *urbs in rure* – a constant succession of people coming to visit you. We come and go a lot. We're not stuck here. And now, when I go to any city, I seek out cathedral, red-light district, sleaze, whatever is funkiest and dirtiest and most threatening, not as a contrast to the country, but because that's where the city is really the city, just as here the country is really the country.

These residences derive from the North American utopian tradition. The longest-established ones are Yaddo and the McDowell colony, which have been there since the twenties and thirties, and are very much part of the thinking which created New Providences and New Blisses and New Hopes and New Havens all over that continent. It's extremely important that there's a turnover so that the ambience of the place constantly changes. The continuity here comes from the fact that we encourage the more successful artists – in the broadest possible definition of the word – to come back, so in any one year, 20 or 30 per cent of the people have come regularly, another 10 or 15 per cent might have been some time in the past, and then something like 50 or 60 per cent are newcomers. Entry is entirely on the basis of people's achievements – not their drinking habits, or their table manners, or their sexual proclivities or anything else. Some people are given the benefit of the doubt when we have our selection meetings: they might publish their book, but wouldn't be offered another opportunity to come until they've actually published, or had the one-person show, or got the film made, or whatever it is. The place isn't an end in itself. There are people who put it on their CVs as if it were an award, but it isn't, it's a leg-up, a help, an act of faith in them, a hope.

Once people are here it's very self-reliant, and trusting. The house makes no impositions beyond making dinner in the evening and expecting that everyone will turn up for it – which they inevitably do. But otherwise, we don't pry, people aren't expected to write reports on what they have done; if they invite me to go and look at their work in the studio, or tell me *viva voce*, or afterwards in a letter or postcard, we're very happy to have that, but we don't expect to be told. As Brian Friel said when he did the opening in October 1981, looking out of the window – and, I always add, scratching your arse – can be part of the creative process.

When Guthrie was thinking what to do with this place, his niece, Julia Crampton, had been to visit a place called the Virginia Center for the Creative Arts, and she it was who put the idea in Guthrie's mind that this would be a good use for Annaghmakerrig, since they had no children. In his will Guthrie left the most broad, generous and trusting wish for the place, which was that it would be 'a place of retreat for artists and suchlike creative persons, who shall have the right to walk over the land, boat or fish in the lake, provided they do not pluck the flowers or interfere with standing crops'. And that's all it says in the will. And there's another little sentence: 'There shall be eight or so at any one time who shall have the necessary equipment to cook for themselves in their rooms, and a hot meal will be provided in the evenings.'

They were the rubrics, and we have developed it from there. In the will, he only left 'my dwellinghouse and its chattels', and not an inch of land outside of it, and that was the difficult part of the inheritance that we've had to deal with over the last fifteen years. He left all the rest of it to his then steward, in an attempt to make reparation for the sins and usurpations of his class. It was a rather Chekhovian will, a bit like *The Cherry Orchard*, in which of course Guthrie was steeped. He lived here in a quite aristocratic but remote way; he had little understanding of the capacity of the Irish peasant for cupidity, meanness, begrudgery, all the things that this particular Irish peasant went on to exemplify once he'd been left essentially master of the place. There have been very trying times because of this battle between the forces of good and the forces of evil. I don't exaggerate when I say that. It really has been a life-and-death struggle for the soul of the place.

In three separate stages we negotiated enough room to garden, to put a ladder up against the house, to prevent the encroachment of this bloody-mindedness on the place itself, on Guthrie's central vision. But Guthrie did have this kink of thinking that these people could be made worthy of The Big House, which he was on the point of giving them before this idea for an artists' retreat came up. Had he done that, this place would be in utter ruins, without a shade of doubt. Because we have come to know these people and what they're capable of, in the way that proletarians from Belfast can know peasants from Monaghan. Very similar mindsets meet.

I grew up in a semi-detached house in a cul-de-sac in Andersonstown, in Belfast, one step up from corporation housing. In my gardening capacity I call myself Capability Brown from Andersonstown. I do the garden here. I also call myself The Janitor. I've come to realize, not having been a custodian of property – either my own or anybody else's – before I came here, that when you love a place as much I've come to love this, and when you become as intimate with it as I am – I go onto the roofs, I have an eye for the gutters, and I hear every sound that might be a bit awry – you absorb the physical place, it becomes part of you. Keeping the house rainproof and warm and decorated and welcoming, and full of the atmosphere of the

a broad, generous and trusting wish

Guthries, is a job in its own right, in which Mary is deeply involved also.

It's a living museum, a microcosm of cultured Anglo-Irish life, which is now acquiring other accretions of this new history that it has, this new family of thousands that has come to live here in the same privileged way that the Guthries and the Powers and the Moorheads lived here; and that extends to every part of the place. That's why it has been so important to re-integrate the estate. We'd like to acquire the remaining two gate lodges, and buy out the forestry leases. If the forestry were an income for the place, as it very well could be, then we would develop other ideas that we have with Marcus McCabe for making a model permaculture set-up, where the creativity of the place would be fed in an oblique way by the land itself, by the woodlands, and the place itself would become the scenario for creative action.

All that is about making the place resonate with what it does, quietly. It doesn't have to make a great deal of public noise because we are generously supported by the two Arts Councils in a very open-minded way. We don't have to be associated with exhibitions or continually prove ourselves. For all its traps and difficulties, Guthrie's will was from the best possible motivation and the highest possible philanthropic principles, so I would imagine they would have encouraged such a use of the place as we have in mind, and particularly as it would create employment, both directly and indirectly, which Guthrie wanted to do when he set up the jam factory in Newbliss. Local people grew the fruit and bought shares in the factory, and the hope was that the young people would find employment there. But Guthrie once again was a bad judge of character, and appointed a local shyster, fly-by-night, son of gombeen ne'er-do-well, against everybody's better judgment; and nobody had the courage to say right out, don't do it. According to Guthrie's sister, Peggy, it was very bad for Guthrie to get that knighthood, because nobody could talk to him after that.

We were having dinner with friends last night, and their teenage daughter wanted to know if I was an idealist. I said, well, I was a member of the Communist youth league in my youth, marcher against the Vietnam war; my first act as an even then unmatriculated student at Queen's University in Belfast was to be in the demonstration after October 1968; I was editor of the student newspaper and various wildly radical gazettes. That was nowhere in my family background. In the Irish context, the seeds of radicalism and idealism come from the 1947 Education Act. Seamus

Heaney and Seamus Deane, and lots of others in that first generation, have acknowledged it as crucial in allowing them to break away from the farm.

There was also the prosperity of the post-war years, and the opportunity to travel, the growth in communications. So that you could be me, as a very incoherent sort of socialist in Belfast, watching *les événements de mai* in *soixante-huit à Paris*, and wanting to be there, and in a way being there, with Rudi Dutschke and Daniel Cohn-Bendit as my proto-heroes. We all absorbed that into ourselves in our own ways, adulterated with whatever mind-changing substances we were having, or whatever other experiences we carried off into the Aquarian conspiracy; it all went down through the cracks in the geo-politico-litho-sphere, and it's re-emerging in people like Bill Clinton and Jerry Rubin – who's now working on the Stock Exchange.

It's a rare privilege to be able to attest your idealism. People simply have to be covert about it, and if they get away with anything, it's little jabs against the establishment, or being able to do something of use for the disadvantaged. What I do isn't art. But to help to sustain a context in which artists can find their own niche, their own milieu, is to participate vicariously in what a lot of us would envy about artists: they work at home, *selon leur propre gré*, they have distinct steps of achievement – publications, exhibitions, etc. – and their work is their pleasure, as well as, of course, their anguish. I know this concept from the Pyrenees, where there's still a residual peasant community in the true sense of the word peasant, as in *paysan*, which is to do with the land. These villages have grown out of the land, they're quarried from the mountainside; work, for the people who live there, is not the obligation that it is in developed society.

We're here for the foreseeable future. But we're by nature vagrants; something else might come, or we might recognize that we no longer have the energy or ideas. We have a house of our own in the Pyrenees, in a village where we've been instrumental in fermenting a centre for art and nature a bit on the model of Annaghmakerrig. We might go there, or elsewhere, or nowhere – sometimes the prospect of living up a boreen and seeing nobody for weeks and months has its allure. But we do have a *modus vivendi* here: we have our own house whose privacy is absolutely respected. There are so few opportunities for people to do absolutely what they want. I see myself doing exactly what I want; this is completely it, for now.

a broad, generous and trusting wish

Johan's front step looks out on a hundred and eighty degrees of land, sea and sky. He has lived here for eighteen years, and has built barns, sheds, workshops and a windmill.

Common sense

There's common sense, uncommon sense and common nonsense. Common sense is the kind of thing you learn when you live on the land – I didn't learn any when I was growing up in Holland. My father did the accounts for a company and everything was very normal, I suppose – very common nonsense – but I was pretty wild. I did a few boring jobs in offices for two or three years, and then one day I was cycling to work – I was nearly there – and I just turned round and went home. I couldn't face it, the job was so stupid, such a stupid way to live, I couldn't handle it at all. I had to go to a doctor – in Holland these things are very well organized – who told me I had a bad philosophy of life and sent me to another doctor who asked me to take my clothes off. I thought he probably just wanted to look at my body, and I refused. I was always very honest.

So by then I was officially disqualified from their life, that is, I was qualified for a pension from the Queen – for life. I didn't have to call to any office or look for a job, they didn't care what I did. A few years later I came here, where you could say this house was waiting for me.

I've been here eighteen years now – eleven years with my wife and my kids, then seven on my own – a long way from those people out there in the post-modern world. When my wife was here we used to have goats, bees and vegetables. In the beginning we grew wheat and ground our own flour; we made cheese from the goats' milk, collected honey from the bees.

It's a very ancient instinct to make the land productive, always to push it a bit further, and plant another row of potatoes, or a rose bush. I never did much to the house, though – the kitchen ceiling is exactly the same as when I first came here – but I made that chair, with the big flat armrest for your drink to sit on. I made my loudspeakers. That drawing of the Eiffel Tower my father gave me when I was ten. It's very faded now.

I made a hut for myself at the end of the hay-shed, just with a bed and a table and chair. I used to go there to be alone. Or I put up a very small tent in the field and look out at the space. Lots of people are completely knocked out by the space, they can't handle it. I'm thinking of building some cabins up the mountain so people can come and stay here. It's possible my pension will stop, and I have to have some way of earning money. I'd build them myself, with a bit of stone, and then I have some wood around the place.

I don't see people very much since my family left, but I cycle into the village every day to buy a few things and meet a few people. I don't know what this solitariness is, but I need to be in a lookout position a lot of the time. This is a powerful place, you know, you're on the edge. One winter, for three months, the wind was never below force five. Oh boy! Very good place for a windmill. Yes. The windmill. Very Dutch! I've been doing it for seven years now. When you're making all the parts yourself it can be very slow. You have to have a lot of energy and concentration. And you have to finish it. Of course it cost a lot of money – the batteries alone were £7000. I had to take out a loan, but everything else I paid for along the way, including my lathe. I eat very simple food, so I save money.

Many of the things for the windmill I invented myself, like this 2CV handbrake on the propeller shaft and the tapered roller bearings from the wheels. The 2CV is the only car I know! I bought the one I'm driving now for £50 twelve years ago, and rebuilt almost all of it. I met people in Holland who rebuild 2CVs. They go to work in the day, and then the rest of the time they build a car – and they're absolute perfectionists. The car they build is much better than the one you would buy. But the 2CV is a very good machine. There's nothing like a good machine.

John Moriarty was born in north Kerry; he taught in Canada then returned to Ireland in 1971, where he has been a gardener and a writer. He now lives near Killarney.

What have those mountains worth revealing?

I taught English literature in Manitoba very happily for six years. I loved teaching, it allowed me to be passionate about things I feel passionately about. In Winnipeg it was easy to get invited to big parties; if you wanted, you could have a good life. It was the 1960s, and you wouldn't need to go to bed lonely. I don't know of a more beautiful society than a North American campus at that time. There was an air of freedom, the formalities and a lot of the savageries had fallen away.

But after six years I felt I needed to go back and then come forward again, to be outside institutions, and even outside civilization. I was glutted with culture; Europe is glutted with culture. The year before I gave up teaching, I'd been in Paris, and for the first few months of the Michaelmas term I was wrestling with it. Will I go on? Will I leave? Then three of my students came to see me just before Christmas and said, We have a transit van and we're going on a big journey around the States, do you want to come? So off I went with them. It was wonderful to go five, six thousand miles in a transit van, to go down, out of the ice age, and eventually hit brown, red earth down below Santa Fe, and we got out of the van and rolled in this red earth. I remember spending Christmas Eve down on the floor of the Grand Canyon, under the Palaeozoic, feeling diminished by the infinity of the space, and wondering: What kind of significance does a human have down here? We went back up through Utah and Montana, and I thought, Christ, my Europeanness has been shaken, this is a really big country and I want to stay. I told everyone I was staying. But then, just before the end of the next term – it was Spy Wednesday – I'd gone home and I was sitting in my chair and suddenly I knew: I'm going. I was thirty-three. I didn't feel that in leaving my job I was doing something courageous. It was more like an anguish: I have to do it, I cannot not go.

I wrote to my brother in Ireland asking him to find me somewhere to live, anywhere on the west coast from Malin Head to Mizen Head. I wanted to rediscover my bush soul, to know what I was, outside the boundaries of my civilization in the woods and the fields. Native Americans say that you have your soul in culture, and then there's your bush soul which is outside culture, outside civilization. One day when I was back in Ireland, I went out to baptize myself, literally, I immersed my head three times in a river. I was supposed to go back three more times but I didn't. My bluff was called. I needed something more than nature.

Emily Brontë has written a poem about going out into the family glen, to leave the old heroic traces, leave history, leave culture. In one stanza she says, 'And what have those mountains worth revealing?' It may be that you will encounter parts that you won't encounter in civilization, and then you will need the wisdom and support of culture. I am hugely and enormously grateful to culture. A book to me isn't matter to read, it's, will it take me through the night? These books that you see around me here have been one way of getting through the night. I'm not reading them as a professor or a critic, I'm reading them because they nourish me.

Though there were extraordinary moments teaching in Canada. I would go down to a lecture hall to teach Keats's 'Ode to a Nightingale', and so we would be on Hampstead Heath where tender is the night, and immediately outside the plate-glass window it was fifty degrees below zero, it was ice-age: out there you die. The collision between Keats's poem and what was outside the window was irreconcilable. English literature doesn't belong in this landscape. It was like a giraffe at the North Pole. You could possibly teach *King Lear*, because you're out of doors, you're out on the heath 'and there's ne'er a bush for half a mile about'. But that sort of language is asymptotic to what was outside the window. The only culture you can teach in Manitoba is what the Indians have. Their myths grew out of this land.

So I was aware that the books I was passionate about – the canon of English literature – couldn't house me in Canada; its metaphors, its images, its insights, its institutions and its solutions, its cadences, weren't able to shelter me. I had that constant sense that culture and cosmos weren't a continuum; whereas if I'd built an igloo and lived from Eskimo stories, lived out circumpolar shamanism, then I would certainly be aware of a continuum of culture and cosmos.

There's no continuum in Europe. The educated European head isn't good for the earth now. My education – particularly in philosophy – turned my head into a web; no wonder I had to baptize my head three times! I had to start again, like the mosaic-maker, but in nature, with individual tesserae – the individual sensations of what my hand felt like in running water, what a sunset looked like, what the leaves on the trees sounded like – and maybe finally arrive at conceptions.

I grew up on a farm – going out for the cows, bringing in buckets of water from the well. I didn't call it a sensuous life, but it was, it was a life of rolling in the earth, swimming in the river and jumping in bogholes, a life of going off raiding other people's orchards. I grew up in a neolithic world. We had no electricity, no radio, we lived by a double-wick lamp. I went to bed in total darkness every night. I was as aboriginal in Europe as any aborigine in Australia. And then one day three tall ships arrived off my aboriginal coast, and, instead of being part of a biblical world, I was part of Darwin's origin of the species; so what happened to the Australian aborigines happened to me.

One of the things that did worry me when I came back to Ireland was, how am I going to do without female company, and of course I discovered that the need wasn't nearly so urgent as it had been in Canada. You were out every day, going out into the country, climbing mountains, running along the top of mountains, sometimes with hailstones against you. All your muscles were delightfully aching, so you were sensuous right throughout your body. The rain against you was a sensuousness, the wind was a sensuousness. The experience of you cycling against the wind or walking against the wind was a sensuousness; you getting wet, you getting cold, just looking at a gravel bed in a mountain stream, it was sensuousness all the time in multifarious ways. The particular kind of sensuousness we call sexual sensuousness wasn't as clamant; the libido was right throughout

what have those mountains worth revealing?

your body, it wasn't as genitally located as it would be in a city.

It was a wonderful, intense and sensuous life. I was wild, I was happy – don't fence me in! And I wasn't being fenced in. It was wonderful, it was crazy and wonderful. And I crashed. I was myself the iceberg against which I crashed. Seeking your bush soul is dangerous. What I did was a bit reckless. I'm not talking heroics; I was doing what I yearned to do, it was impassioned, but I needed to get back to culture again.

Your education would love to turn you into a canal; you're contained within the banks and you move in a straight line from one town to the next, but there's parts of you – and I think there must be parts of everyone – that still want to be wild, to be tumbling down a mountain, to be a river that no one is pushing. When I grew up there was very little control on us; we could be out for five hours and no one would wonder where we were or when we were going to show up. It isn't like that for children any more, even in the country. I would suspect everyone has this wildness in them, but within culture it comes out in a Sid Vicious way, demonically in rock or punk music. The drumming hilarity with which people left the offices in 1914 to do battle indicates that people wanted to get the hell out of civilization and start fighting. There was a tiredness in people – I'm dying inside of civilization: I'm a canal, I don't want to be a canal, I want to be a river, don't fence me in. Think of Rupert Brooke 'into cleanness leaping'.

Most of us are frightened, and we are quite rightly frightened. It's like the sorcerer's apprentice. The sorcerer was away one day, and the apprentice had the formula to summon the spirits, but he didn't have the formula to send them away and quieten them down when he wanted his sleep. Their time isn't your time, and your time isn't their time. So we do need the restraint of culture, we do need the forms of culture, and it is because we need them that they exist.

When I talk about culture I'm not necessarily talking about what passes for culture in the twentieth century; I'm talking about something like the primitivism of the *Tao Te Ching*, the great Chinese religious classic. He'll talk about two villages so close to each other they can hear the cocks crowing and the dogs barking, but they won't cross back and forth from one to another. They don't need to travel. All the culture they need is there in their own little community. I'm talking about culture at that level, the culture of language, the culture of symbols and images and rituals, the culture of being able to cross another person's threshold and read the people within, the graces of culture.

You have to ask, and ask brutally, is my culture, and my way of life in that culture, vampiring me? Is it literally sucking me dry? Or is it nurturing me? All you have to do is stand outside factory gates on any evening and see the people pale as mushrooms coming out, and you say to yourself, they're vampired. If, as a little baby in my mother's womb, I was able to ask that question, is it nurturing me or is it vampiring me, and if I decided it was vampiring me, it was time to get the hell out. But it was nourishing. A culture nourishes you. But a modern culture vampires you. Even in a place like a university, which is much freer, if you look at the people there, they're being vampired – sometimes by their overwillingness to cooperate with the demands of the institution. Vampired is a strong word, but it needs to be strong. You look at some people and they've no blood left at all. You're mortgaged to the financial houses, and you're mortgaged to other people's image of you, and you're mortgaged to your own image of yourself.

If I were teaching now I'd be preparing people for the collapse. I'd be saying to students: Anywhere you look in history, you see huge discontinuities. It is a hunch of mine that in your lifetime you will experience a major historical discontinuity; the modern world will collapse. How will you cope with that when it comes? And the discontinuity has to happen, otherwise we're fecked. Just as people woke up one morning to find the Soviet empire gone, so we'll wake up one morning and find that the capitalist order has gone. When Cortez and his four hundred arrived in South America, the Aztec religion and empire collapsed. This happened in what we call 1619, but the Aztecs called it Year 1, the year of need. We're going to endure our year of need. I would say to students, don't mortgage yourself too much to a collapsing order. It's a giant system of casinos, one in Tokyo, one in New York, one in Paris, the London stock exchange. The casinos are betting against each other. There isn't any kind of stability there.

You stand under a hole in the ozone layer and you ask, where are we going?

Western civilization hasn't got long to run. I'm fifty-eight years old, and I've led in many ways an extremely privileged life, no thought police have ever knocked on my door and, on the evidence of what I was reading, sent me off to the gulag for a pyschiatrist to normalize me. So in a sense

what have those mountains worth revealing?

I've been protected, I know, by armaments, submarines, bombs; the culture of humanity was available to me, which, in terms of the lives of most other people, is a great privilege.

When I look out of my window, what do I see?

Days when the mists come down on the Tomies and on Torc and on Mangerton, and the mist is opening and closing, revealing and concealing, I feel present at the first morning of the world. I don't see what Europeans see when I look at nature, I don't see matter. I've never ever anywhere seen nature as matter, at best I see mind in hibernation. When the bear goes into hibernation you think it's dead, but it's actually alive, and then come spring, it gets up and walks off. That mountain is mind, hibernating for a few geological epochs; it wouldn't surprise me if I woke up one morning and, like a brown bear coming out of hibernation, it had just walked away, like the mists and the clouds it had gone, bang. When I look out there I see big medicine; there's wonderful medicine in nature, but we have to work with it in translation.

The English language suggests that the ego is source of everything: I do, I make, I bring, I fight, I sing. But, do I dream, or does the dream dream me? Or does the dream dream itself independently of me? Does the poem in some way write itself? Keats says that if the poem doesn't come to you as naturally as the leaves fall off a tree, then you'd better not write it. So how do we know why we write? We are bigger than what we are, egotistically, bigger than the individuals we are, much bigger than we are socio-politically or socio-economically. Rimbaud said, *'On me pense'* – someone is thinking me, and a Kalahari bushman says there's a dream that dreams us, and Heidegger says that language thinks us, speaks us. So when we think about writing of a particular order, we're dealing with something completely different from the ego.

When I write an introduction to a book, it's a deliberate, practical piece of writing, like a set of directions to get to Cork. But the other writing has nothing to do with deciding. You were sunk into this seance, which wasn't a trance, you were fully conscious, there was a deep silence, and out of it, you wrote. You wouldn't always know exactly what you'd written at the end of the poem, or the story, only that it was significant.

The fact that I don't depend on civilization in ways that other people do, doesn't mean that I'm not dependent. The older I grow the more dependent I become and the more happily dependent. I'm not heroic; the only courage I now have is my courage to depend. I depend on my neighbours, I depend on their light in the darkness at night, I depend on God, totally, I depend on prayer, on my connectedness to the ground, I depend on a sacramental life to bring me through. You're not alive if you're not dependent on something. You can get married because you need a prop. I haven't done that, I live alone. But this altar table is a prop; that's my baptismal candle, and the Bible; they're all part of Christianity. The bird's nest, eagle feather and falcon feather are North American Indian and represent sacred nature. My aboriginal relationship with animals means the animals will bring their medicine to me. The native North American Indian looks out on the world and doesn't see it as an economic opportunity; he sees the world as big medicine. A bear can come in, an eagle can come to a tree and bring you medicine. I need the medicine that is in nature, as an Indian does. I will find a woodlouse trapped inside the house and take it outside and let it go and say, go back into the world and ask for healing for me.

I had thought of setting up a hedge school here, where people would go off walking in the mountains in the day, and in the evening there'd be a fire they could sit round, and talk, or not talk.

what have those mountains worth revealing?